Gun Notes

Research on Guns

Michael R. Weisser
Mike the Gun Guy™

Volume 9: Guns in America

1

ISBN: 978-0-578-45314-9
LCCN: 2019900824

First edition.

Cover design: Hannah Spencer, Nineteen Pieces, LLC.

In Memory: Jean & Saul Weisser

2

Contents

Preface	Page	4
1. Guns – Benefit or Risk?	Page	5
2. Understanding Gun Violence	Page	31
3. Understanding Gun-Violence Data	Page	49
4. Where Are the Guns?	Page	62
5. Guns and Gun Violence	Page	78
6. Regulating Guns	Page	104
7. John Lott	Page	127
8. Gun Laws and Gun Violence	Page	141
9. Murder and Guns	Page	159

Preface

I come to the issue of guns from both a practical and scholarly
background, but the issues I choose to explore are always shaped by my
research and the research of others.

Over the last several years, I published 8 research papers with the Social
Science Research Network. This volume pulls them together and gives me
the opportunity to revise and rewrite various parts of those papers - one
should never view a piece of research as a closed book.

I also read the work of other scholars, as well as discuss their work and my
work both through emails and face-to-face. What follows is an alpha
listing of some of the researchers who have shared their time, thoughts
and data with me.

Deb Azrael – Cathy Barber – Philip Cook – Jahan Fahimi – Eric Fleegler
– Kristin Goss - David Hemenway – Daniel Kahan – Bindu Kalesan -
Gary Kleck – John Lott, Jr. - Matt Miller – Andrew Papachristos -
Frederick Rivara – Ali Rowhani-Rahbar – Michael Siegel – Jeffrey
Swanson – Daniel Webster – Frank Zimring.

There are others, too. My appreciation and thanks to everyone, named and
unnamed.

Study 1 - Are Guns a Benefit or a Risk?

This debate began with the 1998 publication of *More Guns, Less Crime,* a book in which John Lott argued that homicide rates correlated with possession of right-to-carry (RTC) licenses, leading to a decline of homicides in localities which issued RTC. His argument was initially critiqued by John Donohue in a Yale Law review of Lott's book, and the two adversaries have been going at it ever since.[1]

The disagreement between Lott and Donohue is much more than the usual academic argument which remains hidden in arcane, scholarly journals or is the occasional subject of a panel discussion at an academic conference attended by nobody other than other scholars working in the same field. This is because the issue of whether armed citizens should and can protect themselves and others from crime has become a contentious and extremely vituperative discussion in the public domain. In fact, more than any other issue, the risk versus benefits of armed, self-defense define the gun debate today.

In 1970, when the American civilian arsenal probably amounted to roughly 110 million guns, less than one-quarter were handguns, most of which were the old style, long-barreled six shooters carried by the good guys and bad guys who shot up the OK Corral.[2] More than half of American households held a gun, but for the most part these were shotguns and rifles used for hunting or protecting livestock from predators and 'pests.'

As America became an urban and suburban society, hunting began to give way to other forms of recreation and outdoor sport, with a consequent decline in demand for products like long guns which no longer served the needs of a population not living on the land. In 1986, American gun makers produced 3 million guns, of which half were handguns; since 2000 handguns have accounted for more than half the new guns going into the commercial firearms market each year.[3] Were it not for the growing popularity of assault-style rifles over the last 15 years, the proportion of handguns to long guns coming out of gun factories would be roughly three to one.

This product shift took place at the same time that research on gun violence first appeared linking higher fatal injury rates from penetrating trauma to the availability of guns. Foremost in this respect were studies by Arthur Kellerman and Frederick Rivara, who found that households containing guns experienced much higher deaths than households where guns didn't appear.[4] This research was then generalized into a wider perspective by David Hemenway, who correlated gun access with excessive rates of fatal violence in the U.S. as compared to all other countries in the OECD.[5]

The narrative that gun ownership was the primary factor in elevating gun injuries to what Katherine Christoffel calls the 'endemic' state of American gun violence, was a challenge to the gun industry whose defense was first taken up by the criminologist, Gary Kleck. In 1995, Kleck published the results of a telephone survey, and based on 222 responses, claimed that people used guns to thwart upwards of 2.5 million criminal acts each year.[6] Only 15% of these 'defensive gun uses' (DGU) involved actually firing the weapon at another human being; most were events in which the person who otherwise might have been a crime victim let it be known that he or she could defend themselves with a gun.

Kleck's paper became the basis upon which the gun industry began to shift the marketing of its products away from hunting and sport to using guns as a response to violent crime. Taken together with the research by Kellerman and Hemenway, what emerged was an argument which I refer to as an argument about the social utility of guns. Either guns represent a positive social utility (protection against crime) or they represent a negative social utility (high rates of gun violence) – Americans must choose.

What John Lott has contributed to this debate about the social utility of guns is to take Kleck's argument to another level and attempt to prove the validity of positive social utility based on changes in the rate of violent crimes. Lott's main argument in his 1998 book, *More Guns, Less Crime*, was that violent crime rates, particularly murder, declined because criminals did not want to test Kleck's DGU thesis and switched their behavior from in-person to anonymous crimes.

Lott's book and the attendant publicity which his thesis received, along with extremely positive accolades from the pro-gun lobby, has made him known as the "most prolific and influential writer on gun violence," a description coming from a gun violence prevention (GVP) blogger, who was certainly not pleased at having to write those words.[7] It was seductively easy to cast Lott as the chief villain in America's switch from long guns to handguns, with the consequent increase in gun violence, because when his book appeared, he became something of a fixture on pro-gun media shows, the decline in murder rates that he associated with the growth of RTC licensing was gathering steam. Lott's data originally covered the years 1977 through 1994, a period when the violent crime rate grew from 475.9 to 713.6, most of this increase a function of murder and aggravated assault. By 1998, however, the violent crime rate had dipped to 523.

The Donohue-Lott Argument Begins.

Leaving aside for a moment Lott's explanation for this decline, the question of why the United States experienced a nearly 50% drop in

7

violent crime between the early 1990's and over the next twenty years, has provoked one of the most extensive and exhaustive academic debates perhaps Henri Pirenne blamed the shift of Western Civilization from the Mediterranean to North Europe on the appearance of Islam in a little book, *Medieval Cities*, published in 1927. But as provocative as Pirenne's argument was to medieval historiography, it had no impact on political affairs. That simply cannot be said about the current debate over the decline of crime. To quote a summary of the debate's importance, "It melds law, economics, science, criminology, and public policy analysis to address the challenges facing our country."[8] That's quite a debate.

Whether he's right or wrong or somewhere in between, Lott's book is a fundamental milestone in that debate. The point at which he and Donohue first crossed swords was over the latter's attempt to explain the crime decline, an attempt that provoked significant controversy far beyond anything written by Lott.

In 2000, Donohue and Steven Levitt published a paper, "The Impact of Legalized Abortion on Crime," which may be one of the most prolifically-discussed and debated scholarly articles in all of the social sciences, not just as regards the issue of the crime decline.[9] Levitt went on to fashion an entire scholarly career and a considerable personal fortune with the development of his personal brand of economic inquiry and methodology known as 'freakonomics,' which takes seemingly disconnected phenomena, links them together through regression analysis and then explains how and why things happen the way they do.[10]

As a species, humans have an innate desire not only to understand the world around them, but to predict how and when that world will change. Using observations of any type of behavior to predict if and when that behavior will change is an inexact science at best, not only because if we could predict the future it wouldn't be the future, but also, because our observations about anything are a function of the manner in which we

8

choose to gather data on past events. Not only do we choose how to gather the data, we also choose what kind of data to gather, both procedures fraught with inexactitude relative to the conclusions that we derive.

In this regard, using various regression analysis models to explain crime is a particularly fertile method to generate an academic debate, if only because we tie so many socio-economic indicators to the behaviors usually assumed to produce criminal activity in the first place. And while scholars always posit the idea that criminal behavior is complex and multi-faceted, the whole point of regression methodology is to reduce this complexity to a gradation of causes, allowing us to identify the most essential issues for which mitigating strategies can then be designed.

Precisely because criminal behavior is a function both of multiple environmental as well as sociological factors, regression analysis is frequently used to illustrate the complex relationships between criminal causalities, even if the understanding of the interactions between these causalities may not be fully understood. This is the reason why Lott, for example, broaches the issue of causality at the very beginning of his book (p. 27) because he knows that any attempt to impose a unilateral explanation for variations in crime rates may prove to yield answers that cannot necessarily be sustained.

No such qualms appear to have affected John Donohue and Steven Levitt when they ascribed the drop of violent crime in the 1990's to one, specific event which took place twenty years before. Rather than adding the effects of legalized abortions (thus reducing the numbers of 'unwanted' children who otherwise would have been neglected and therefore more likely to grow into a life of crime) to the other accepted causalities for the decline of crime, D&L state that Roe v. Wade accounted for 50 percent of the drop in violent crime – no other scholar has ever posited an explanation for the post-1990 crime decline which relies so heavily on only one, specific causal event.[11]

The argument put forth by D&L is an attempt to explain what they refer to as 'the recent abrupt improvement in crime.' The only problem with this narrative, however, is that the improvement (or decline) in crime rates was certainly abrupt but was also short-lived. In fact, by the time the abortion article was published in 2000, the crime declines which began in 1990 had flattened out by 1998 and would fall roughly 2% a year from then until 2016.

If, as D&L propose, crime rates correlate positively with abortion rates, indeed correlate much more strongly than any other variable, how do they explain the fact that the increase in reported abortions which reached its post-1973 level in 1990, then began a steady decline following that date, did not result in more unwanted children came into the world, as alternatives to abortion such as contraceptive measures, became more widespread?[12]

Any decline in criminal activity is obviously first and foremost a function of how many individuals decide to commit crimes. D&L places this estimate at roughly 3% of any age cohort, a number based on the study of a single age cohort; i.e., male children born in Philadelphia in 1945.[13] They take this number, then assume that children born out-of-wedlock are most likely to fall into the crime-prone category, then find a decline in abortions, hence a decline in out-of-wedlock children being added to the general population, thus creating a prime facie connection between abortions and crime.

Building an argument in this fashion isn't a scientific methodology, it's guesswork backed up by statistical packaging which may create a bunch of dots but doesn't connect them in any meaningful way. I am hardly the first reader to review the D&L abortion article from this perspective, but when the piece was reviewed by John Lott, he stood D&L's entire argument on its head, producing a statistical analysis which supported the contrary argument, namely, that access to legal abortions created more crime, particularly homicide crimes.[13]

The purpose of this paper is not to discuss the disagreement between Donohue and Lott over whether legal abortions did or did not impact violent crime rates in the decades following Roe v. Wade. I point it out because the same argument is now made by Donohue against Lott, namely, that redrawing the data results in Lott's basic argument about the relationship between crime rates and the issuance of RTC being reversed; i.e., the more RTC licenses in the general population, the more violent crime goes up! Before I get into the details about Donohue's critique of the Lott thesis, however, the reader deserves a brief overview of what Lott really says and doesn't say.

The Lott Thesis.

Like the abortion paper of Donohue and Levitt, the work by Lott connecting RTC issuance to crime rates is also a contribution to the larger argument about the decline of crime. But Lott's approach and the choices he made about gathering data differ from D&L in two important respects: First, D&L only used a basic category of 'violent crime' along with some limited usage of homicide data to understand the impact of legalized abortion, whereas Lott broke violent crime into its four constituent categories (homicide, aggravated assault, rape and robbery) and tested his assumptions about the impact of RTC against each one. Second, D&L only looked at the abortion-crime connection following the legalization of abortion access, first in 5 pre-Roe v. Wade states, then throughout the

11

country following the 1973 decision. On the other hand, Lott tested his thesis with a before-after comparison of states which issued RTC.

By differentiating between specific violent crime trends, Lott gives us a much more nuanced view, both of the decline in crime starting in the early 1990's, as well as what led up to the reversal of crime rates which had climbed steadily from prior to the period he covers beginning in 1977. I have calculated the entire sweep of overall violent crime from the late 1960's through 2015 and the overall trend (using rolling 5-year averages) looks like this

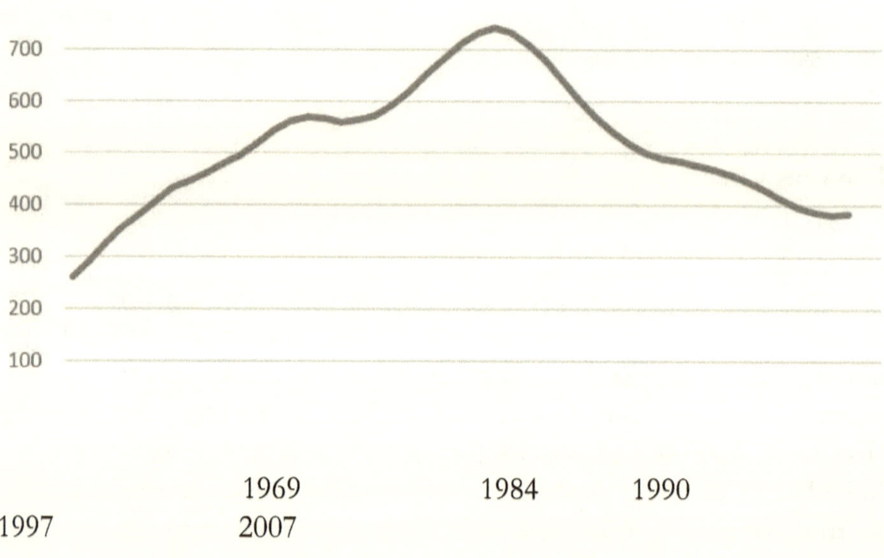

When we break violent crime into its constituent parts, the trend-line changes in different ways. Here is the trend for assault (orange) and robbery (blue):

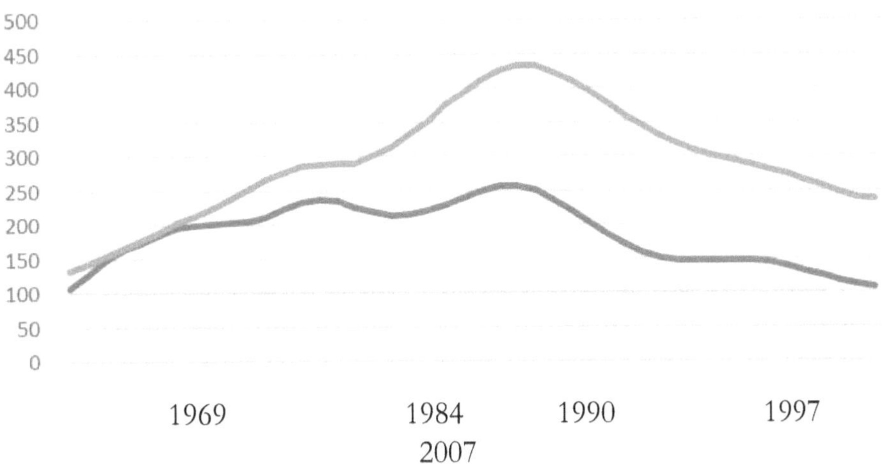

Note that when we examine trend lines for aggravated assault and robbery, that the former begins a steep rise after 1982, whereas the latter remains basically unchanged during the great crime increase of the 1990's, but then shows a significant drop between 1991 and 1996. Thus, the 'abrupt' change found by Donohue and Levitt in violent crime holds true for aggravated assault but not for robbery crimes.

Now we turn to murder and here's what we find:

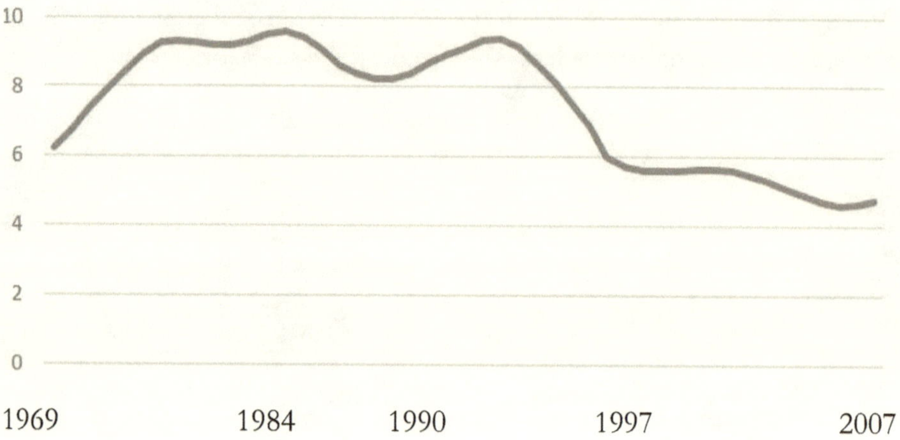

For murder, we have an unprecedented increase from 1965 until 1971, then a waffling and finally a downward slip until 1982, then another rise until 1989 followed by a sharp decline which ends in 1996. What appears to be the crime category most responsible for the overall violent crime trend between 1965 and 2015 is aggravated assault, a category which Donohue doesn't mention at all in his abortion study or his critiques of Lott, whereas Lott finds no statistically significant connection either way between aggravated assault and RTC.

Because Lott finds his strongest connection between RTC and the movement only of homicide trends, he adjusts his theory to account for this correlation by presenting a rather novel explanation based on the idea that criminals in localities which issue RTC switch their criminal behavior away from face-to-face crimes, preferring instead to engage in anonymous criminality (burglary, auto theft, etc.) because there is less chance they will encounter a crime victim who happens to be armed. While this explanation may be consistent with the behavior of different criminal categories matched against RTC as the causal variable, I am not sure that one can easily assume that the type of criminal behavior which produces homicide could be consciously altered to make it more likely that the same individual will commit a different kind of crime.

One thing which appears to be present in just about every criminal act resulting in the victim's demise is that the behavior of the attacker is random, impulsive and rarely, if ever planned.[14] On the other hand, crimes like burglary require at least a modicum of thought and planning before the act takes place. Therefore, to assume that someone can make a rational and thoughtful decision to substitute anonymous criminal behavior like burglary, for face-to-face criminality as in homicide, is to make an assumption that is nothing more than a leap of faith. The fact that burglary declined at a much slower rate than homicide after 1990, doesn't necessarily prove any kind of substitution effect.

I'm not being entirely fair to Lott in this respect because my graphs above capture only national crime rates, and Lott is careful to distinguish between RTC and crime at state and county levels, the connection between these two trends often masked when data is aggregated in national terms. This is a particularly important nuance to bear in mind because much of the crime epidemic which began in the mid-1980's and then abruptly turned downwards in the early 1990's occurred in large, metropolitan areas which were not usually jurisdictions that granted RTC either before, during or after the period in which the most obvious crime-rate changes occurred.

Notwithstanding my reservations about Lott's approach to the issue of the great crime decline, I believe his work deserves serious consideration, and should not be viewed as simply an effort to put a scientific gloss on some kind of apologia for the gun industry. In Donohue's critique of Lott that I will examine in detail below, Donohue states that Lott's work "may well have encouraged state legislatures to adopt RTC laws," when in fact, by the time the first edition of *More Guns, Less Crime* appeared, more than 30 states had already adopted 'shall issue' RTC statutes, reflecting a grass-

15

roots movement initiated in Florida more than a decade previous to the appearance of Lott's book.[15]

 Condemning Lott's work as an example of false or misleading narratives which promote gun ownership and the value of guns for self-defense has become a cottage industry within the gun-control community, an example being this statement from a popular gun-control blog: "After every mass shooting or national gun violence tragedy, Lott is the de facto talking head for the pro-gun community on news programs such as Fox News. He has also testified numerous times in front of Congress and state legislatures, having been a critical voice in the expansion of Right-to-Carry (RTC) laws."[16]

Like the rationale advanced above by Donohue as a motive for attacking Lott, this statement also flies in the face of reality regarding how and when Americans began accepting the positive social utility of guns as a response to crime. In 1959, Gallup conducted a national survey based on the following question: "Do you think there should or should not be a law that would ban the possession of handguns, except by the police and other authorized persons?" This question effectively broached the basic difference between gun policies in the United States versus every other OECD country, namely, free access to handguns. In 1959, positive responses were 60%, negative responses were 34%. In 1999, shortly after Lott's book was published, positive responses to the same question were 34%, negatives were 64%.

By ascribing to John Lott's work a formative role in the growth of pro-RTC sentiment, gun-control scholars and advocates are saying something which is simply not true. If anything, what Lott has managed to accomplish since his book first appeared is to build a public persona by recognizing and taking advantage of shifts in public thinking about guns, shifts which began to emerge well before he was a known personality in

16

this field. I will return to this issue following my analysis of Donohue's latest anti-Lott work.

The Donohue Counter-Thesis.

 In 2017, Donohue updated his earlier critique of Lott by extending the data to cover the period 2000 – 2014 and subjecting the data to a different regression model known as 'synthetic controls.' Basically, this method allows researchers to predict the result of a change in a causal variable (i.e., issuance of RTC) by comparing the consequent result (i.e., crime rates) between localities which did, as opposed to did not affect the change.[17] It is argued that the synthetic control approach advances the value of regression methodology because it makes regression analysis a more robust tool for predicting, as opposed to only describing changes in trends over time.[18]

To take advantage of the comparative methodology embodied in synthetic controls analysis, Donohue created three state groups: one group adopted RTC laws between 1977 and 2014, the second group adopted RTC prior to 1977 and the third group never adopted RTC. What he and his research colleagues found was that the decline in violent crime rates in non-RTC states was between four and five times higher than the decline in violent crime found in states which adopted or already issued RTC.

Having produced this finding based on simply comparing crime rates in RTC versus non-RTC states, Donohue now takes a leap of faith and states that "the synthetic controls analysis best supports the view that the adoption of RTC laws substantially raises overall violent crime in the ten years after adoption"[18] Except this evidence actually shows this to be the case only if we accept the idea that the main driver of criminal behavior is the existence of RTC laws. Voila! Abortion as the *deus ex machina* of crime trends is now replaced by RTC.

I would be somewhat less skeptical of this explanation were it not for the fact that by compiling the three groups of states differentiated only by the existence or non-existence of RTC creates a bias in evaluating the comparative outcomes between the different groups that Donohue appears to not only neglect, but not even be aware of how this bias could shape his results. What I am referring to is the fact that of the eight non-RTC states (I am excluding the District of Columbia) two of these states – California and New York – together constitute nearly 40 million of the 59 million residents of the entire non-RTC states. Which means that what happens in those two jurisdictions alone will determine the overall outcome for that group as a whole.

And what happened in those two states beginning in 1993 was a decline in crime, most notably in the major urban centers, which was not only unprecedented in national terms at the time but continues to the present day. Los Angeles set a record for yearly homicides in 1992 with 1,092 murders, most committed with guns. That same year New York City recorded 2,020 homicides, a decrease of 134 from the year before. These two localities alone accounted for 20% of all U.S. homicides in 1992, their combined populations counting for 4% of the entire U.S. population. By 1998, the national murder rate had dropped by 29%, but in New York City the decline was more like 70%, in Los Angeles the drop was slightly more than 60%.

 If these two cities experienced such an enormous drop in murders due to the non-issuance of RTC, how do we explain the fact that these same two cities previously found themselves facing gigantic increases in murder rates, given their non-issuance of RTC? Does Donohue ever ask how come his use of synthetic controls to explain crime rates only works if crime is going down? But that's not an issue we need to consider, since the
18

explanation for upward movements of crime indices has already been furnished by Donohue with his work on abortion and crime.

 Comparing the trends on murder to other violent crimes (p. 12 above) note how different the former is from the latter. Murder increased sharply in the late 1960's, then began to level off and actually declined at the same time that robbery and assault were beginning to grow. Murder rates crested in 1989, other violent crimes continued an upward trend through 1991 (using five-year averages.) Then all three crime rates experienced a drop but the decline in murder was much quicker and much more pronounced.

The extent to which murder rates differ from other violent crime rates as well as the overall rate of violent crime should alert us to another problem in Donohue's counter-argument against Lott, namely, the degree to which what he claims to be differences in crime between RTC as opposed to non-RTC states is not based on comparisons between actual criminal occurrences. In fact, it is a comparison of predictive trends assuming that the synthetic controls used to replicate the interplay of various causal factors would hold true as one goes beyond the time-frame for which data actually exists. In this respect, Donohue builds a case around what might happen to crime rates in RTC versus non-RTC states; Lott builds his case based on what has already occurred.

Lott's work not only distinguishes between the different crime categories, whereas Donohue only looks at murder rates in specific terms; Lott is also aware of the degree to which state-level crime data often distorts or disguises more than it explains, whereas Donohue only utilizes state-level data in both the comparisons and conclusions he draws about the causality of RTC. To a certain degree, Lott's utilization of county-level evidence also creates problems insofar as many counties with limited populations cannot furnish conclusive evidence on crime rates because even the appearance of a single criminal incident could generate a significant change

19

in the rate of crime. While Lott at least acknowledges these issues, Donohue passes over this issue as if it doesn't even exist.

I would still be willing to give Donohue's argument the benefit of some of my own doubts were it not for the fact that, at the conclusion of his article, he moves entirely away from data-driven analysis and issues an arbitrary, gratuitous and totally subjective editorial on the cause of gun violence that has nothing whatsoever to do either with the content of his work or any verifiable, evidence-based data at all. I am referring here to his statement about what he believes to be a link between gun violence and RTC issuance based on violent behavior of RTC-holders themselves. I quote Donohue at length:

While this paper has focused on the statistical estimation of the impact of RTC laws, it is useful to consider the mechanisms by which RTC laws would lead to net increases in violent crime; that is, the statistical evidence shows us that whatever beneficial effects RTC laws have in reducing violence, they are outweighed by greater harmful effects. The most obvious mechanism is that the RTC permit holder may commit a crime that he or she would not have committed without the permit. A number of high profile crimes by RTC permit holders would seem to follow this pattern: George Zimmerman, the popcorn killer at a Florida movie theater who was angry at a father texting a babysitter, and the angry gas station killer(shooting a black teen for playing loud rap music) are all individuals who would likely never have killed anyone had they not had an RTC permit.[19]

Of the three 'high-profile' killings cited by Donohue to support his theory about the risk of granting RTC, one of the killers happened to be the retired head of the Tampa SWAT team (the 'popcorn' killer) whose 28-year, unblemished law enforcement career certainly entitled him to walk around with a gun. As for the idea that RTC recipients commit violent crimes far beyond the number of crimes which do not occur because people are walking around with guns, there is simply no evidence which Donohue can cite that would back this argument up.

The Violence Policy Center reports that between 2007 and 2017, some 700 shooting events occurred in which someone with RTC either shot and killed themselves or someone else. We can discount 40% of these events because they were suicides, which do not constitute a criminal threat of any kind. Of the remaining 500+ killings committed by RTC-holders, obviously the numbers aggregated by the VPC are no doubt underestimated, but even if we were to double or triple the number of RTC shooting events, as a factor in the overall incidence of gun violence, it wouldn't count at all.

Donohue attempts to compensate for what he knows to be low numbers of shootings by RTC-holders by fashioning an explanation which can only be considered a shot in the dark (pardon my pun.) Again, I quote Donohue at length:

Some have questioned whether permit holders commit enough crime to substantially elevate violent criminality, citing apparently low rates of social withdrawals from permit holders convicted of crimes. Two points need to be made in response to this claim. First, official withdrawals clearly understate criminality by permit holders. For example, convictions for violent crime are far smaller than acts of violent crime, so many permit holders would never face social withdrawal of their permits even if they committed a violent criminal act that would warrant such termination. Moreover, social withdrawals will be unnecessary when the pending permit holder is killed. In the nightmare case for RTC, two Michigan permit holding drivers pulled over to battle over a tailgating dispute in September of 2013 and each shot and killed the other. Again, without permits this would likely have not been a double homicide, but note that no social action to terminate permits would ever be recorded in a case like this.

The second critical point is that RTC laws also increase crime by individuals other than permit holders in a variety of ways. First, the culture of gun carrying can promote confrontations. Presumably, George Zimmerman would not have hassled Trayvon Martin if Zimmerman had not had a gun. If Martin had assaulted Zimmerman, the gun permit then could have been viewed as a stimulant to crime (even if the permit holder was not the ultimate perpetrator). The messages of the gun culture can promote fear and anger, which are emotions that can invite more hostile confrontations leading to more violence. This attitude may be reinforced by the adoption of RTC laws.[20]

My response to Donohue's two points are as follows. First, for someone who buttresses his arguments throughout his work with reams of data and sophisticated statistical analysis, the entire issue of threats posed by the RTC population suddenly is devoid of even the slightest reference to evidence-based information of any kind. The anecdote involving the 2013 dual homicide in Michigan involving two RTC-holders is an interesting and somewhat unique example of road rage, but it says absolutely nothing about whether or how often RTC licenses are revoked or suspended in instances where the licensee may have committed a serious crime.

Donohue's second point about RTC creating a culture in which armed citizens are less likely to back down or avoid a confrontation leading to violence is certainly an issue which needs further study and I suspect such studies might well prove Donohue's idea to be correct. But what I find interesting in Donohue's argument about the aggressive culture promoted by RTC, is that he seems to believe that such culture only exists in the minds of people walking around with guns.

Going back to the 'popcorn' shooting mentioned above, the two principals who engaged in the dispute were seated one behind the other in a movie theater which, at the time of the shooting, contained less than 30 patrons in a theater holding more than 400 seats. Following Donohue's argument, we must assume that only the ex-cop was ready to escalate the argument because he was carrying a gun. When he was asked to stop texting, why didn't the unarmed man move to another seat where he could have continued texting to his heart's content? Instead, he not only told the ex-cop to f*ck off, but then threw a bag of popcorn at the man who told the Court that he thought the pop[corn might have been a gun.

We seem to be living in a society in which backing down has nothing to do with whether or not someone is armed. On August 9, 2014 in Ferguson, MO Michael Brown did not have a gun when he responded to a cop's demand to back off by coming forward and escalating a verbal dispute into a physical assault. Why does Donohue feel it appropriate to only consider the issue of aggressive behavior when it involves someone with a gun?

Is There a Donohue-Lott Synthesis?

If there were grounds for basic agreement between Donohue and Lott, as well as between the two constituencies whose views they embody in their work, there certainly has been enough time and ink spilled to bring this controversy to an end. The fact that these two capable scholars have been engaged in this dispute for more than two decades with no sign of compromise on either side tells me that the grounds for agreement are non-existent to microscopically thin.

But while I have tried to be as objective and honest as possible in describing what I believe to be the most salient features of the debate, I find myself more in agreement with Lott's argument than with the argument which Donohue makes. And I say this for the following reasons.

First, I do not share Donohue's evident attempt to shape his work so that it will counteract what he believes to be Lott's influence over the growth of armed, self-defense culture, as well as the legal strictures that promote

23

that cultural view. And I say this having written numerous articles on my own blog and elsewhere condemning the gun industry for promoting armed, self-defense and RTC, because I do not believe that citizens should take upon themselves the responsibility of community safety through the use of guns.

Second, Donohue knows full well that his use of the synthetic controls method does not really alter the degree to which his estimates about the impact of RTC are exactly that – estimates, without any real grounding in facts. When he says that "our analysis suggests that had states avoided adoption of RTC laws, they would have experienced greater drops in violent crime," he is basically saying that his regression methodology cannot define the relationship between crime rates and RTC beyond an educated guess. Meanwhile, he has no trouble justifying the guesswork based on the idea that his results can "reliably guide policy in this area."[21]

With all due respect to the attempts by Donohue and others to use the results of their research to guide policy, in a policy area as fractious and divisive as gun control, the last thing we need is to be guided by suggestive conclusions about what might work or might not. It would be one thing if Donohue and like-minded scholars would develop a synthesis which could actually explain whether and to what degree armed citizens do or do not constitute a crime risk; it is quite another to produce a suggestive explanation as a byproduct of the continued effort to diminish or denigrate the argument made by the other side.

Gun-control scholars, led by John Donohue, continue to entertain themselves by dismissing Lott as a misguided fool, an intellectual crank or worse, while public opinion continues to shift towards accepting Lott's argument and rejecting the findings which 'suggest' that he is wrong. Lott's public presence doesn't make him the leader of a national movement to promote gun 'rights;' his work simply validates decisions made by a majority of Americans that a gun represents a benefit, not a risk. This majority includes many people who don't own guns, and I fail to see even the slightest attempt on the part of gun-control scholars to understand how or why this cultural shift has come about.

I would like to offer up a suggestion to Donohue and his scholarly colleagues for how they might begin to develop a serious research synthesis that might actually serve both as a guide to successful policy-making in this area, as well as begin to create an alternative narrative about gun risk that could be attractive to the public at large. I note that Donohue's article begins with an acknowledgement to 17 individuals who aided in the analytic work that went into creating the article itself. What I find interesting is that not one of the people named and thanked by Donohue and his co-authors has ever published a single bit of gun research themselves. In other words, to the extent that Donohue took advantage of the resources and talents of other experts, their expertise did not extend to anything related to the scholarly research about guns.

If Donohue and other like-minded scholars are really determined to seek an end to the behavior which results in 120,000 Americans being killed or seriously injured each year (along with many more who suffer the psychological trauma of witnessing these events) they could take a tiny fraction of the ink they have spilled criticizing John Lott and use it to sharpen their arguments among themselves. And the way you do that is to critique each other's work in the public domain, rather than reserving your published criticisms to take an academically approved pot-shot at John Lott. I have never read a single word of criticism about Donohue's work in the gun-violence field. Even Albert Einstein had to content numerous published criticisms of his work after the General Theory first appeared.

To quote the brilliant Marxist economist Paul Baran: "An intellectual is thus in essence a social critic, a person whose concern is to identify, to analyze, and in this way to help overcome the obstacles barring the way to the attainment of a better, more humane, and more rational social order."[22] And being a social critic means criticizing everything in one's environment, most particularly the work of colleagues whose research creates the intellectual context within which one formulates their own research ideas.

So, the question comes down to this. Do gun researchers want to behave like intellectuals or not? Are they so wrapped up in their efforts to 'guide' gun-control policies that they are unable to step outside the narrow orbit of advocacy and conduct research based solely on the search for truth? The biggest problem facing gun-control advocates is the degree to which many of their strategies are fixed by what Tversky and Kahneman refer to as 'anchoring,' i.e., beliefs that are fixed by initial explanations about a problem and then become resistant to any significant degree of change.[23]

What troubles me most of all about the reaction of Donohue and others to the work of John Lott is that their efforts do little, if anything, to dislodge the gun-control movement from its anchored beliefs. Which means that the only thing we can rely on to alter the basic landscape of the gun debate is the public reaction to the mass slaughters which now appear to be occurring at a record pace. This is a rather unfortunate state of affairs and gun-control scholars might ask themselves whether their efforts have contributed to how this situation has come about.

NOTES

1.Ian Ayres and John Donohue III, "Review: Nondiscretionary Concealed Weapons Laws: A Case Study of Statistics, Standards of Proof, and Public Policy," American Law and Economics Review, I, 1-2 (Fall, 1999), pp. 436-470.

2. F. Zimring and G. Newton, Jr., Firearms and Violence in American Life (Maryland: NIJ, 1969). Re-posted in G. Kleck, Point Blank, Guns and Violence in America (New Brunswick, Aldine, 1991).

3. Department of Justice, ATF, "Firearms Commerce in the United States, Annual Statistical Update, 2017," (2016.)

4. A. Kellerman, et. al., "Gun Ownership as a Risk Factor for Homicide in the Home," New England Journal of Medicine, 1993, 329 (October 7, 1993) pp. 1084-1091. This article has produced its own bibliographical pile, some of the articles interesting, many unfortunately silly.

5. E. Grinshteyn and D. Hemenway, "Violent Death Rates: The U.S. Compared with Other High-income OECD Countries," American Journal of Medicine, 129, 3 (March, 2016), pp. 266273.

6. G. Kleck and M. Gertz, "Armed Resistance to Crime: The Prevalence and Nature of Self-Defense with a Gun," Journal of Criminal Law and Criminology, 86, 1 (Fall, 1995) pp. 150- 187.

7. E. DeFilippis, "Shooting Down the Gun Lobby's Favorite 'Academic,': A Lot of Lies," www.armedwithreason.com, December 1, 2014.

8. O. Roeder, et. al., "What Caused the Crime Decline," Brennan Center for Justice, (2015), p.2.

9. J. Donohue, III and S. Levitt, "The Impact of Legalized Abortion on Crime," NBER Working Paper 8004 (November, 2000).

10. There have been endless discussions about Freakonomics, positive and negative, but a balanced summary of Levitt and Dubner's works was published in The Guardian blog: Michelle Dean, "Freakonomics 10 years on: Stephen J. Dubner and Steven Levitt on what they got right and wrong (May 15, 2015).

11. Cf., a summary of all the credible 'crime decline' arguments in the Brennan article cited above (fn. 8).

12. https://www.guttmacher.org/news-release/2014/us-abortion-rate-hits-lowest-level1973.

 13. John Lott and John Whitley, "Abortion and Crime: Unwanted Children and Out-of-Wedlock Births" (2001). John M. Olin Center for Studies in Law, Economics, and Public Policy Working Papers. Paper 254 (May, 2001.)

14. I believe the single most authoritative discussion about the motives behind homicide still remains an article written by Lester Adelson, whose 1,000-page forensic textbook on homicide remains an absolute classic, as does this piece: "The gun and the sanctity of human life; or the bullet as pathogen," Archives of Surgery, 127 (June, 1992) pp. 659-664.

15. Brian Anse Patrick, Rise of the Anti-Media, Informing America's Concealed Weapons Movement, (Toledo, 2013).

16. E. DeFilippis, op. cit.

17. John Donohue, et. al., "Right-to-Carry Laws and Violent Crime: A Comprehensive Assessment Using Panel Data, the LASSO, and a State-Level Synthetic Controls Analysis," NBER (June, 2017.)

18. ibid., p. 44.

19. ibid., p. 45

20. ibid.

21. ibid., p. 3.

22. P. Baran, "The Commitment of the Intellectual," Monthly Review (February, 1961.)

23. A. Tversky and D. Kahneman, "Judgement under Uncertainty: Heuristics and Biases," Science, Vol. 185, 4157 (September 27, 1974), pp. 1124-1131.

Study 2 – Understanding Gun Violence

The idea that the United States suffers from an unusually high rate of fatal violence because of access to guns is hardly new. It was first remarked upon by Franklin Zimring in 1969 and has been a watchword of the gun violence prevention (GVP) movement ever since.[1] Here's the defining statement from the Brady Campaign: "The U.S. firearm homicide rate is 20 times higher than the combined rates of 22 countries that are our peers in wealth and population."[2] The reference for this statement is tied to a peer-reviewed article published in 2010 by Erin Grinshteyn and David Hemenway (hereafter referred to as G & H) updating research done by Hemenway and others covering data through 2003.[3]

The idea that the exceptional level of fatal violence experienced by the U.S. is a function of the availability of guns has become ingrained in the basic messaging of the GVP movement, as well as defining GVP strategies for bringing the homicide rate down. Since private gun ownership in America is a constitutionally-protected right, the GVP movement has responded to the findings which show a link between gun access and violence by promoting various strategies to keep guns out of the 'wrong hands;' i.e., certain types of individuals are more prone than others to use guns to commit injuries and assaults. Thus the idea is to develop policies and procedures that will identify such individuals and restrict their access to guns.

The problem with such an approach, however, is that while 120,000-or more gun deaths and injuries each year appears to be a formidable number, far beyond what occurs in any other advanced nation-state, it represents a very small amount of the behavior which creates most firearm injuries each year. According to the FBI Uniform Crime Reports, more than 800,000 Americans are arrested each year for aggravated assault; i.e., someone intentionally tries to attack someone else with the intention of inflicting serious bodily injury that could result in death.[4] The National

Crime Victimization Survey, on the other hand, which builds its data on queries of more than 225,000 households annually, sets aggravated assaults at more than 1 million plus domestic assaults at another million or more. This same survey puts gun 'victimizations' (a gun is witnessed during a criminal event but not necessarily discharged) at somewhere around 400,000, although the FBI sets actual criminal gun use at 75,000 or slightly higher.[5]

Let's accept for the moment that virtually all of the illegal or inappropriate behavior that elevates our level of lethal violence above that of everywhere else is the result of guns getting into the 'wrong hands,' wrong either because the individual should never have been allowed to have access to a gun in the first place, or wrong because a particular gun owner always behaved in a proper way until the moment he decided to yank out his gun. But when we say that there is a connection or what public health researchers refer to as an 'association' between guns and violence, what are we really talking about? This is not just an issue of incomplete data, it also requires us to understand both the advantages and limitations imposed by using regression analysis to explain the causality of parallel events; a problem which becomes more complicated when we are talking about violence, which in the greater scheme of human behavior is still a rare event.[6]

The public health researchers who have created the argument about access to guns being linked to high rates of violence are aware of the degree to which the data on violence can be misused as easily as it can be used. Thus, while they argue that the overall violence rate in the U.S.A. is no different from what is experienced in other OECD national states, they also use the data covering only fatal violence as a basis for making their argument about the impact of guns. Defining gun violence only in terms of fatal gun injuries has the virtue of at least avoiding the pitfalls caused by the fact that there is no definition of aggravated assault which fits every legal system in an analogous way, but when it comes to homicide, it's difficult to hide a lifeless body no matter where you are. Furthermore, the

32

G&H research avoids entirely the definitional discordance between criminal as opposed to health data, because it is based on the WHO ICD10 classification system, which is uniform wherever it is applied.

Here are the basic findings from the 2010 G&H report:[7]

- The firearm homicide rate is 25 times higher and the firearm suicide rate is 8 times higher in the United States than in other high-income countries.
- Among all 23 countries, with less than half the total population, the United States accounted for 82% of all firearm deaths.
- Ninety percent of women, 91% of all children aged 0 to 14 years, and 92% of youth aged 15 to 24 years who were killed by firearms were in the United States.

Utilizing ICD classifications not only allows researchers to diminish if not eliminate definitional discrepancies of criminal violence in different countries, but also allows for more precise measurements to understand the differences in violence rates occasioned by the availability of guns. When we differentiate between overall homicide rates and gun-homicide rates, however, the degree to which the United States is so exceptional among high-income countries begins to fade away.

Examining the argument.

Of the 23 countries for which G&H collected data, only the United States had a gun homicide rate (per 100,000) of 1.0 or more in fact, the U.S. rate was 3.6.8 No other OECD country had a firearm homicide rate of more than 0.5 (Canada and Portugal) and 16 of the remaining nation-states had rates of 0.2 or less.

When we examine rates representing non-gun homicides, however, this great disparity is no longer so great. The United States is no longer the outlier, it's non-gun homicide rate of 1.7 is exceeded by the Czech Republic (2.4) with Hungary (1.4) and Republic of Korea (1.3) not far beyond. As opposed to the gun-homicide rate in OECD countries, where 16 nation-states had little to no gun-violence at all, 7 countries had rates at least 50% of the U.S. rate, and not a single country had a rate of 0.2 or less.

This difference between gun-homicides and non-gun homicides is used by G&H to bolster their argument about the degree to which gun access drives overall homicide rates, an argument made by Hemenway, in a previous article published in 2000 article cited above, albeit without the much more accurate data used for the updated research published in 2000. The fact that overall violence rates in other OECD countries are higher than gun-violence rates thus becomes the non-plus ultra explanation for the disparity between our level of fatal violence and fatal violence everywhere else.

The only problem with this argument is that while the data supports the conclusion; that gun access promotes lethal violence, is that the entire approach to the problem rests on several definitional and methodological assumptions which often serve as guides to research on the epidemiology of injury, but do not necessarily provide a firm foundation for understanding injuries caused by guns.

 Research on how and why product injuries occur usually explore two questions simultaneously. (1). Did the injury occur because the product was used in a dangerous way that was not anticipated during the process of product design? (2). Did the injury occur because the consumer operated the product in an unsafe way? In many cases such as automobiles, the injury turned out to be a function of both. In some cases, such as cribs with bars set too widely apart, the injury was more a function of the former; in the case of bicycle helmets, the latter event (falling off the bike) is what caused the injury to occur.[9]

34

When it comes to gun injuries however, particularly fatal injuries, neither of these assumptions hold true. Guns first appeared in China at some point prior to Marco Polo's 13thcentury visit, when the Chinese figured out that by igniting a mixture of potassium nitrate, ground charcoal and sulfur one could produce an explosion which generated gas pressures great enough to propel a solid object through space. The trick, of course, was placing the solid object into some kind of device which would be aimed at a target that the solid object would then hit. Voila - the cannon was invented, a contrivance which was adopted by European armies by the 14th Century and brought the Middle Ages to a close.

The only difference between the ancient cannon (pictured above) and the handgun that has just been adopted for use by the U.S. Army (pictured below) is that we have figured out how to reduce the size of the weapon and figured out how to load the weapon in a much more efficient way.

Believe it or not, in the seven centuries since Western armies first started using the cannon in warfare, the basic reason that the mechanics of guns really haven't changed is because the gun is designed to do one thing and one thing only, namely, to make it easier and quicker to commit physical harm – the point being that a gun functions properly and is being used properly when the result of its use is an injury either to the user or to someone else.

The reason why the public health template used to understand product injury doesn't fit well when it comes to guns is because the only way one could redesign how a gun functions or how it is used would be to turn it into something other than a gun. Thus, public health gun violence researchers usually end up falling back on the second assumption, namely, that gun violence can be reduced if we figure out how to change the behavior of the individuals whose inappropriate or illegal behavior results in the injuries caused by guns. Unfortunately, this assumption also doesn't fit very well.

The Uniqueness of Gun Violence.

To better understand this issue, we need to look more specifically at the behavior which results in one person ending the life of another, because this behavior is not fully understood and this lack of understanding compromises many of the studies and conclusions about fatal violence resulting from the use of guns. To begin, alone among all criminality, murder is the rarest event. Note that this paper refers to 'murder' even though legally-speaking such behavior is categorized as 'homicide,' so that we can distinguish between murders committed aggressively as opposed to murders which are properly the result of self-defensive behavior on the part of civilians or the police.[10]

On average, between 2010 and 2016 there were slightly less than 17,000 murders committed each year. Meanwhile, during those same seven years, roughly 1,200,000 violent crimes resulted in arrests each year, with the total number of actual violent crimes probably rising annually to 2 million or more. Since the number of murders reported by the CDC is perhaps the only accurate number covering any category of violent crime, we can assume with some degree of certainty that murders account for less than 1% of all violent crimes committed each year. In other words, murder is an extremely rare event, so rare in fact, that in 2014 more than half of all the counties in the United States did not report a single murder at all.[11]

Not only is murder a very rare event, but we know next to nothing about the relatively small number of individuals who decide to commit murder by using a gun. This population constitutes roughly 70% of the population who kill someone besides themselves, so as a percentage of people who commit serious violence, it is even a smaller number than the less than 1% who take violent behavior to its ultimate extreme. The basic difference between people who kill without using a gun as opposed to people who kill by using a gun, however, is the latter method is very efficient and has a much greater degree of success than hitting someone with a club (blunt trauma) or slicing them with a knife (penetrating trauma) which happen to be the most common methods for killing people other than using a gun.[12]

For the years 2013 – 2015, the CDC counted 185,586 intentional assaults with guns of which 35,195 were homicides; in other words, gun assaults ending in death accounted for 16% of all intentional gun injuries committed by one person against another. During the same period, deaths from intentional cutting/piercing (code X99) amounted to 5,001, intentional cut injuries were 386,961; intentional cutting deaths accounted for slightly more than 1% of all intentional injuries where the weapon was a blade. As for intentional injuries caused by hitting or some other type of assault which did not involve a weapon, there were 3,962,187 such events recorded by the CDC from 2013 to 2015, of which 341 resulted in deaths.

As this chart demonstrates, using a gun to commit the greatest level of injury is far more efficient than any other method that can be employed:

Type of Assault	Fatal	Non-Fatal	Total	% fatal of all assaults
Firearm	35,195	149,991	185,586	0.1896
Cutting/piercing	5,001	381,960	386,961	0.0129
Non-weapon	341	3,961,846	3,962,187	0.0000861
Totals	40,537	4,493,797	4,534,734	0.0089

The Specifics of Fatal Gun Violence.

Why aren't more assaults committed with a gun? With perhaps as many as 300 million or more guns in the civilian arsenal, it certainly cannot be the case that getting one's hands on a gun would constitute a difficult undertaking, particularly in regions of the country (the Southern states, the Western states) where most residents own one or more guns.[13] The relative absence of guns from most acts of violent behavior also cannot be understood as a reflection of guns as being only available to persons above the minimum age for gun ownership because the age cohorts most frequently represented in acts of gun violence and all acts of violence happen to be the same.

The degree to which guns are rarely used in assaults, as opposed to any other method of inflicting injury, can best be explained by understanding the socio-behavioral factors that generate assaults, as well as the specific behavioral decision-making process which occurs in gun assaults and sets those events apart from every other type of assaultive event.

Assaults reflect the transition from non-physical to physical anger which has not been channeled into more appropriate and less dangerous behavior. Overwhelmingly, anger and aggression spill over into violence when an individual either can no longer channel the anger felt towards someone else in less physical ways, or decides to express the anger by committing a violent act against someone who might not be directly connected to the issues that created the anger in the first place.

Either way, even though we know that certain factors in someone's circumstances or personal history are 'red flags' for provoking violence, the point at which the actual violent behavior spills out is rarely, if ever predictable as to the exact time or place. What is entirely predictable, on the other hand, is that committing violence with a gun is the only type of intentional injury in which the perpetrator must move through a series of conscious acts prior to arriving at the moment when the act of gun violence actually occurs.

First in this chain of behavioral decisions involves the decision to get a gun. This is a decision unlike any other decision involving access to a consumer product because guns are the only consumer product for which ownership, access or use requires legal qualifications not found in any other consumer product of any kind.

What is often not understood in the debate about gun ownership is that the same prohibitions which apply to purchasing a gun also apply with
39

equal force to owning or even putting one's hands on a gun. Thus, the decision to give oneself access to a gun first requires understanding the laws regulating gun access and a further decision if it turns out that a particular individual does not meet the legal requirements for gun ownership. In the latter case, the non-qualified individual who decides to go ahead and acquire a gun is guilty of a federal (and usually state) felony even if the weapon in question is never used or even touched at all. To avoid criminal liability, the gun will have to be hidden from view and use by others, it can only be carried outside of one's personal space at even greater risk of being found.

Whether one is legally qualified or not to be a gun owner, acquisition of the gun must then be followed by acquisition of ammunition, another consumer product whose purchase and/or ownership must meet the same legal requirements (along with carrying the same noncompliance penalties) that must be met for owning a gun. Legal or not, the presence of a gun also raises the risk of misuse and serious injury if the weapon is not secured and falls into the wrong hands – children, a mentally-challenged or mentally-ill individual, etc. Studies on the risk of guns in homes where they are present as opposed to homes where guns do not exist, definitively show that a gun in the home increases the possibility of intentional or unintentional injury to the gun owner as well as to others in the home.[14]

On the other hand, gun-violence researchers make a fundamental mistake by addressing the issue of gun injury as if it is just another category in the ACH-10 classification system, to be compared to other types of intentional or unintentional injuries in terms of frequency or other criteria utilized in epidemiological analyses of health risks. If nothing else, using a gun to commit or an injury assumes that the user has invoked a chain of decisions which go far beyond any comparable behavior involving any other way in which an injury might be delivered against someone else.

Were it the case that gun assaults required no more planning or forethought than other types of intentional injury, analyzing and comparing gun violence rates using the standard epidemiological method (number of events ÷ total population) might make sense. But precisely because intentional gun injuries are so unique in terms of what goes into the decision-making process before the injury occurs, to assume that such behavior can be analyzed as something common to the behavioral profile of the entire population is to employ an assumption which completely distorts the reality of violent gun use in the United States.[15]

One other important factor needs to be considered when comparing gun violence to other types of injuries classified as medical events. As is clear from the previous several pages, it is simply impossible to understand gun violence unless one can analyze the behavior of the individual who commits the violent act. Yet the overwhelming public health research on gun violence primarily treats the victim as the end result in and of itself. It really does no good to tell us all kinds of demographic details about the individuals who suffer gun wounds, because that doesn't necessarily tell us anything about who or why someone decided to attack someone else with a gun. And if the whole point is to create an epidemiological model which can help understand and protect the community against a public health threat called gun violence, the threat isn't posed by the person who suffers the injury, it is posed by the person who pulls the trigger of the gun.

We have a number of studies which tell us details about who owns guns, the latest being a very comprehensive study from the Harvard-Northeastern group which gives us a pretty good idea about who owns guns, how many they own, what kinds of guns comprise their personal arsenals and whether their primary reason for owning a gun is for sporting use or personal defense.[16] But I know of no study which asks gun owners whether they ever committed a violent act with one of their guns.

The problem is that we have scant evidence on how intentional gun injuries actually occur because the data utilized to create the epidemiology of this type of injury doesn't link the person who suffers the injury to the person who uses the gun. Clearance rates for gun homicides are somewhere around 70%, convictions for aggravated assault with a gun are substantially less. The CDC data covering injuries doesn't tie victim to perpetrator, neither does the FBI-UCR data tie perpetrators to the persons that they attacked. In order to describe the location of gun injuries we are forced to use only vague, jurisdictional entities like counties or states

The limitations on data which actually explain what happens before and during an act of gun violence is what forces researchers to fall back on generic causal explanations linking fatal violence rates to nothing more specific than the number of privately-owned guns.[17] That being the case, the argument is over before it begins. This is because no other OECD country has the scantest degree of per capita gun ownership compared to the USA, and more to the point, we are the only OECD country that grants free access to handguns, which are the type of gun used almost universally to commit gun violence against someone else. Canada, for example, has roughly one-third the number of per capita guns as its neighbor to the South, but private handgun ownership is basically unknown in Canada, hence a per capita comparison based on population between the United States and Canada has little relevance at all.

The Comparison Between the U.S. and Other High-Income Countries.

The argument about the link between gun-violence rates and guns changes dramatically however, if we compare the number of gun homicides not to the overall population, but to the number of available guns. The reason I believe this to be a much more realistic method for understanding the causality between guns and fatal violence is because guns are not equally distributed throughout the United States; they tend to be much more frequently found in certain localities than others, there is also a marked geographical differentiation between legal versus illegal guns, and most of all, there is a very great difference in the degree to which gun fatalities occur in certain places but not in others, all of these factors having been studied and validated numerous times.

42

We do not have such data for any other country in the OECD, but what we do know is that in no country other than the U.S. does the per-capita ownership of guns approach even a fraction of what exists here. Of the high-income countries listed by G&H, not a single country contained more guns per capita than one gun out of three residents, half had civilian gun stocks which on a per capita basis worked out to one gun to four residents or less. Only the United States has a per capita gun ownership rate of nearly one to one.

Calculating a gun-violence rate based on overall population, the countries considered to be 'high-income,' according to G&H, look like this:

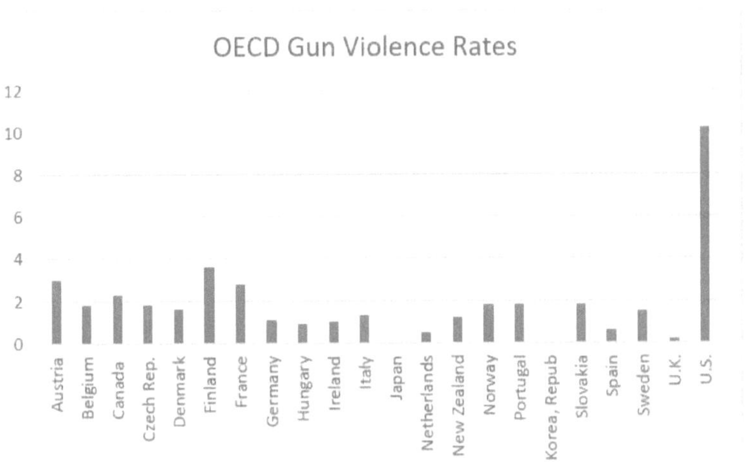

When we calculate gun-violence rates based on the size of the civilian arsenal in those same countries, however, the numbers change to this:

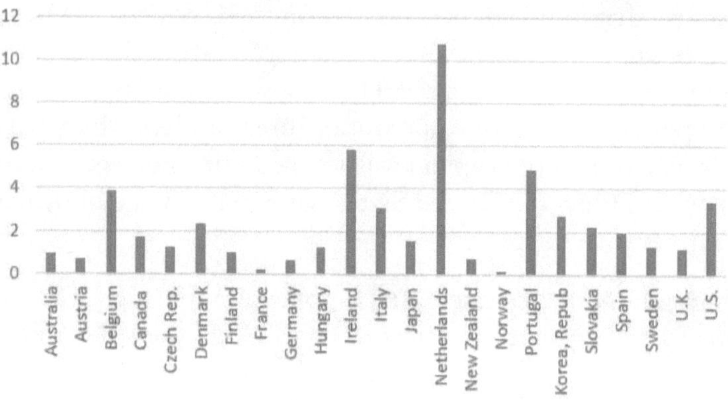

Conclusion

This latter comparison between the U.S. and other countries forces us to frame the discussion about the causal relationship of guns to gun violence in a more nuanced way, shifting from simply analyzing the epidemiology of violence to a discussion about how guns are actually used. If we believe that gun violence is primarily a function of how and when guns get into the 'wrong hands,' then clearly the possibility of guns moving from 'right' to 'wrong' hands is much greater in many other countries than within the United States.

This finding doesn't mean that we should abandon efforts to strengthen laws that keep guns from being accessed by individuals whose behavior and history elevate their personal degree of risk, but it does raise the possibility that this approach needs to be supplemented by other assumptions on which attempts to reduce gun violence are based, rather than simply assuming that the number of guns floating around in the civilian population is the prima facie reason for violence caused by guns.

In the expanded list that I created for a cross-national comparison, the United States accounts for 65% of all gun murders. True, in the high-income countries studied by G&H, the U.S. accounted for 68% of civilian-owned guns, but also accounted for more than 90% of all gun murders. At the same time, the odds that a gun would be used improperly or inappropriately in other high-income countries is greater in many countries than within the United States.

If anything, comparing fatal gun violence between the United States versus other nation-states based not on overall population but on the size of the civilian gun arsenal demonstrates that American gun owners, gun violence numbers notwithstanding, behave remarkable safely with their guns.

NOTES

1.Cf. the 1969 report produced by Zimring for the Eisenhower Commission, Firearms & Violence in American Life, then updated and expanded in, F. Zimring and G. Hawkins, Crime Is Not the Problem, Lethal Violence in America (New York: Oxford University Press, 1997

2. http://www.bradycampaign.org/key-gun-violence-statistics.

3.Erin Grinshteyn and David Hemenway, "Violent Death Rates: The US Compared with Other High-income OECD Countries,2010," The American Journal of Medicine, 129 (2016), 266273; the earlier, research was published as D. Hemenway, et.al., "Firearm Availability and Homicide Rates Across 26 High-income Countries," Journal of Trauma, 49 (2000), 985-98

4.Data from FBI-UCR 'Crime in America' annual report.

5.Cf., https://www.bjs.gov/index.cfm?ty=pbdetail&iid=6166.

6.I have been guided here by the work of Richard Bork and others regarding both the strengths and weaknesses of regression methodologies.

7.G & H, (2016) op. cit., p. 267.

8.ibid., p. 271.

9.Cf., D. Hemenway, While We Were Sleeping: Success Stories in Injury and Violence Prevention (Berkeley, University of California Press, 2009).

10.F. Zimring, When Police Kill (Cambridge: Harvard University Press, 2017). In particular Part I, Chapter 6.

11.https://crimeresearch.org/2017/04/number-murders-county-54-us-counties-2014zero-murders-69-1-murder/. I thank Dr. Lott for helping me understand this data on a very granular basis.

12.All injury data from: https://www.cdc.gov/injury/wisqars/index.html.

13.D. Azrael, et. al., "The Stock and Flow of U.S. Firearms: Results from the 2015 National Firearms Survey" Russell Sage Foundation Journal of the Social Sciences, Vol. 3 no. 5 (2017), 3857.

14.Anglemyer, A., et. al., "The accessibility of firearms and risk of suicide and homicide victimization among household members," Annals of Internal Medicine, 160 (2014), 101-110.

15.I believe that anyone who studies gun homicide should take the time to read the classic forensic homicide textbook by Lester Adelson, The Pathology of Homicide. I could not have approached the entire issue of gun violence absent the many clarifications and insights I gained from this brilliant work.

16.Azrael, "Stock and Flow," op. cit.

17.Here I must take exception to the increasing use of 'open sources' (digital media) to provide data on gun violence. I am not convinced that open-source aggregators like Gun Violence Archive and Mother Jones are necessarily providing workable, verifiable data on which evidence-based, gun violence research should proceed, particularly when scholars who claim to rely on such sources do not furnish the slightest details about the manner in which they used such materials to support their work.

Study 3 - Understanding Gun-Violence Data.

In order to do research on gun violence, we are forced to use data from two very different sources – medicine and law enforcement. This is because more than 85% of all gun injuries, fatal and non-fatal, start off being considered as both medical and criminal events.[1] And even after an initial investigation reveals that slightly less than 15% of all gun injuries are accidents, or what is referred to as 'unintentional' events, and another 15% are suicides, this still leaves more than 70% of all gun injuries to be dealt with both by physicians and the police.

Current public health research on gun violence refers to its epidemiology; i.e., understanding where, when and how gun violence events take place.[2] There is also a subset of this research which predates most of the epidemiological approaches to the problem that attempts to analyze the costs of gun injuries and gun deaths.[3] This paper will deal with the data used to study gun-violence epidemiology.

It should also be pointed out that public health research on gun violence is not an abstract affair; it is conducted in the hopes that such research will provide "an action agenda for academic public health around the firearm injury crisis."[4] The purpose of this paper is to determine the extent to which the data currently used to formulate arguments which advance this 'action agenda' are sufficient to help define and drive such an agenda forward.

The Method.

Medical information about injuries treated in hospitals is published annually by the CDC. The data is aggregated at the national and state level by the National Center for Injury Prevention and Control and can be accessed in two data sets, WISQARS and WONDER, the latter described as being useful for "epidemiological research."[5] Both databases categorize every type of medical event stemming from an injury by using the standardized, ICD-10 system, which is the 10th version of the International Classification of Diseases published by the World Health Organization, a.k.a. WHO.[6]

The first problem one encounters in using the medical data on gun violence is that of all the types of injuries tracked by the CDC, injuries stemming from violence are the only such medical events in which the victim is not usually the individual whose behavior caused the injury to occur. Every other injury category (fire, exertion, car accidents, drug overdoses, etc.) the data covering the victim (age, race, location) is basically all you need to know.

If the injury was caused by the misuse or faulty design of a consumer product, such information is collected by another CDC agency whose work I will review below. But injuries caused by assaults cannot be understood unless one can match up data on both the person who was hurt and the person who committed the assault. No such information is collected anywhere within the CDC.

Before I talk about the implications of doing epidemiological research on injuries when you have no idea how the injury actually occurred, there is a further issue which needs to be addressed even if we confine the research to only knowing about the victim of such medical events. And this issue consists of the fact that gun injuries, both fatal and non-fatal, are, statistically speaking, 'rare' events. Despite all the hue and cry whenever a mass shooting takes place (Las Vegas, Parkland, et. al.) the ordinary, everyday, hum-drum shootings which add up to 125,000+ gun injuries each year, don't occur with enough frequency in many places to allow for a statistically-representative analysis to be conducted at all.
50

In 2016 the CDC reports that 231,991 persons died from some kind of injury and another 32,074,270 were treated in hospital ER units for non-fatal injuries and released. Of the 230,991 fatal injuries, 37,863 were caused by guns. On the non-fatal side, 116,414 gun injuries were treated, bringing the number of fatal and non-fatal gun injuries to 154,277, out of a total number of 32,306,261for injuries of every kind. In other words, guns were involved in 4/10ths of one percent of all injuries – that's a pretty rare event.

Public health researchers will immediately respond to those numbers by saying that gun violence is usually considered a significant public health and medical issue notwithstanding the scant numbers, because it occurs with much greater frequency among certain, well-defined populations and communities, and also creates significant mental and psychological impacts on the entire country when it takes the form of one perpetrator but many victims, e.g., Las Vegas, Columbine, Parkland or Sandy Hook.

Thus, despite its statistically 'rare' occurrence, gun-violence researchers approach the issue on an epidemiological basis, but define their methodology in a rather unique way. Normally, epidemiology starts with studying the illness which causes the public health threat by identifying its initial host, how it spreads, and what environmental factors aid or impede its spread. Once this task has been accomplished, the epidemiologist:

- Counts cases or health events, and describes them in terms of time, place, and person;
- Divides the number of cases by an appropriate denominator to calculate rates; and
- Compares these rates over time or for different groups of people.[7]

Following this methodology, public health researchers have definitively established that the pathogen whose existence will then lead to a public health threat called 'gun violence' is the gun. Even though I have

differences with the degree to which research shows a clear linkage
between gun access and gun violence, no rational individual would deny,
counterintuitively, that gun violence will not occur without the presence of
a gun.

The problem with this approach, however, is that less than 15% of all
medical events defined as instances of gun violence in 2016 involved the
interaction of the pathogen (gun) and only the host (victim).[8] In every one
of the other 132,131 fatal and non-fatal injuries caused by guns, the lack of
information about the transmitter of the pathogen, the shooter, reduces
any epidemiological finding about gun violence to nothing more than a
well-qualified guess.

The Data.

There are two types of medical injuries whose numbers form the basis for
tracking gun violence: fatal and non-fatal. Both injury categories are
divided between 'intentional' and 'unintentional' events. With the
exception of suicide, the former events are also tracked by law-
enforcement agencies and aggregated by the FBI, because most intentional
gun injuries are also assaults. In 2016, the CDC states that there were 495
fatal gun accidents and 21,219 non-fatal gun injuries, for a total of 21,714
unintentional gun injuries, or 14% of all medical events involving the use
of a gun. While 21,714 may sound like a large number, slightly more than
30 million unintentional fatal and non-fatal injuries were treated by
physicians in 2016, an annual number which has held steady since 2010.

Unintentional, non-fatal gun injuries, on the other hand, jumped from
17,311 in 2015 to 21,219 in 2016, whereas accidental gun deaths have
dropped by nearly 20% over the same period of time. How do we explain

a two-year increase of more than 20% in unintentional, nonfatal injuries while fatal gun accidents appear to be going down?

Let's start by describing how and where the data for both types of injuries is generated and then published by the CDC. The unintentional gun death number comes from the same source for all deaths reported by the CDC – death certificates filed at the state level which are then used by the Census, along with birth certificates, to figure out the national population between the actual census count that only happens every ten years. The birth and death numbers are collected by another CDC division, the National Center for Health Statistics, which publishes an annual health national report and then and distributes the data to other CDC divisions, including the folks who push the data into two electronic databases – WISQARS and WONDER – which I discussed above.

In the previous paper I discussed in detail the difficulties in using CDC versus FBI-UCR data for determining valid numbers for homicides caused by guns.[9] Unfortunately, when we examine the issue of intentional, non-fatal shootings, which happen to constitute more than half of every type of medical injury caused by guns, the data is derived neither from medical sources or law enforcement agencies. This information comes from an agency known as the National Electronic Injury Surveillance System (NEISS) which is operated by the Consumer Injury Protection Commission, an agency established by Congress in 1972 whose mandate includes a requirement that they do no reporting on gun injuries at all.[10] This restriction does not, however, prohibit NEISS from collecting information on gun injuries as just another type of product injury, then transferring this information to the CDC.

I have read virtually every peer-reviewed, public health study on gun violence, many of which discuss issues and findings related to non-fatal gun injuries, and I have yet to see any mention of the source of the number on intentional, non-fatal gun injuries except a citation to the

53

CDC. Obviously, the people who manage the CDC injury websites go further into details than what is published by NEISS, for the simple reason that NEISS cannot itself publish any data about injuries caused by guns. But using the NEISS data as if it adheres to the same standards and collection criteria utilized by the CDC for other medical events creates an impression about the validity of information on non-fatal gun assaults which is simply not the case.

As I said above, the numbers used by the CDC to track fatal gun injuries come from death certificates aggregated by state health authorities and then forwarded to the feds. The CDC numbers for gun murders may, in fact, be 20% higher than the possibly more accurate numbers collected and published by the FBI, an issue which I discuss at length in Chapter 9. The difference between medical and law-enforcement numbers for gun homicides, albeit substantial, is nevertheless not as great a concern since gun homicides account for less than 15% of all intentional gun injuries; thus a thousand more or a thousand less gun deaths won't change overall gun violence numbers all that much.

On the other hand, as I pointed out above, given the fact that non-fatal gun assaults account for at least half of all gun violence, both intentional and unintentional, coming up with reliable numbers for this particular category should be an important and ongoing task. When one begins looking at the manner in which the NEISS gun-violence data is collected, however, substantial problems immediately appear.

To begin, NEISS data is based on reports from 100 participating hospitals, grouped by the number of annual visits to each hospital's ER. Out of a total number of 5,388 hospitals which operated emergency departments in 2000, 3,179 hospitals had annual ER visits of between 1 and 16,830, another 1,059 hospitals counted ER visits between 16,831 and 28,150 visits, a further 674 hospitals had 28,151 to 41,130 visits and 426 hospitals had more than 1,130 ER visits per year. The NEISS team classifies these
54

hospitals as Stratum I through Stratum 4 and bases their national estimates on numbers from 48, 14, 9 and 23 Stratum I through Stratum 4 hospitals respectively. They also take data from 8 children's hospitals regardless of the number of ER visits at those locations.[11]

These participating hospitals all agree to furnish NEISS with immediate and ongoing data covering all ER visits caused by an injury from the use or existence of a consumer product. The reports sent to NEISS not only describe the usual patient demographics, but also contain details about the type of product, its manufacturer, model and description, and a concise statement as to how and why the injury occurred. The reports also cover, in particular, whether the injury was based on product malfunction or produce misuse. This data is then aggregated and published each month by the Consumer Product Safety Commission (CPSC) website; it is also used to alert product manufacturers about possible safety defects that might need to be remedied in product design.

When you stop to think about it, exempting guns from CPSC coverage may appear to have been a fillip granted to the gun industry to help boost production and sales, but in another sense, I don't understand how the CPSC could have been required to regulate guns insofar as the regulatory legislation calls for alerting consumers and manufacturers to product defects which make a particular item unsafe. How could you define a gun as being 'unsafe' when its purpose is to create harm? After all, the individual who shows up in an ER with a bullet wound is proof that the gun which was used to create that wound is functioning in exactly the way it was designed. For that matter, unintentional injuries are rarely caused by a gun's malfunction; almost invariably the reason why someone accidentally shoots themselves or someone else is nothing more than, 'duhhh, I forgot to check if it was loaded.'

In addition to the mission of the CPSC as being contrary to the whole nature, design and use of guns, there is also the issue of whether the hospitals used for building the NEISS database could give us an accurate picture of gun injuries, even if the picture is only based on a sampling of hospital sites. I twice asked the NEISS administrators to send me a listing of the participating hospitals, made it clear that my interest was for basic research and that I would comply with any restrictions which might apply to how such information could be used or shared. Both requests were politely and quickly denied.

The reason I asked for the actual list of participating hospitals is that NEISS publishes a handbook for researchers using their data which contains a map of all hospital sites which looks like this:[12]

How anyone could assume that these hospital sites could furnish data which could then be used to create valid sample of gun injuries is beyond me. Note that the participating hospital in Chicago is one of the small hospitals, which means that it probably sees nothing except a small

56

number of slight gun injuries, certainly none of the intentional gun injuries which outnumber unintentional, non-fatal injuries by a measure of four or five to one. Note that there are no participating hospitals in Kentucky, West Virginia, New Mexico and Colorado, states which all show significant levels of gun violence every year. Note that the only participating hospital in Virginia is far away from Richmond, a city which is suffering through a true epidemic of gun violence in 2018. Note that all the participating hospitals in Florida are located in areas of fairly low violence rates yet there is not a single hospital reporting injury from gun-happy counties like Duval, Broward or Dade.

No wonder that when the CDC reports the annual numbers on intentional gun injuries, the 'confidence limits,' meaning that the number could actually be higher or lower, is set at an astonishing 35 percent! In other words, although the 'official' number of intentional, non-fatal injuries in 2016 was announced as 116,414, the real number might be closer to 140,000 or maybe down around 90,000 or even less.13

Implications.

Using primary data whose accuracy may be cause for concern would not be such an important issue if the results of the research remained as nothing more than another contribution to an academic debate. In this regard, I am reminded of a celebrated academic debate known as the Pirenne Thesis, in which a large group of historians, archivists and archeologists argued about the reasons why the center of Western Civilization shifted away from the Mediterranean – a debate initiated by some lectures delivered by a Belgian medievalist, Henri Pirenne, in 1922.

Ultimately, it didn't really matter why the locus of Western political, social and economic development shifted from Rome to Paris beginning in the 7th Century, A.D. The debate made for numerous publications, tenures and promotions at various universities, the usual stuff that happens when a group of scholars decide to argue amongst themselves about this or that historical point.

But when public health and medical researchers delve into the data and produce an argument about the why, how and when of gun violence, this isn't just some kind of esoteric, academic debate. Much of this research is published in peer-reviewed journals, the journals have access to a wide range of public media to spread the word about what new public health findings have come out, the media's narrative then becomes the stuff with which the gun-control advocacy community creates and promotes its narratives for what needs to be done.

I did not write this report in order to besmirch or in any way cast doubt on the work and dedication of the gun-violence research community, of which I happen to consider myself to be a member, no hesitations whatsoever. I wrote it because I believe that academic researchers engaged in this field sometimes do not appreciate the degree to which their work is used not only to build a consensus on what gun violence really means, but also to develop and promote effective policies which will reduce gun violence, an ongoing public health problem which appears to be getting worse.

But the research not only will be used to define the problem as well as possible solutions; it will also be used to gauge the relative value and success of different policies whose specific strategies will be tied to changes in the data being used to justify this policy or that. Which is all the more reason why researchers need to take their audience seriously and state explicitly whether the data they are using can be trusted or not.

58

What it gets down to is whether public health researchers who study gun violence are willing to behave like intellectuals, or are they just trying to preserve their stations in the academy, regardless of whether or not what they produce contributes to the common good. To quote Paul Baran, an intellectual has to undertake a "ruthless criticism of everything that exists, ruthless in the sense that the criticism will not shrink either from its own conclusions or from conflict with the powers that be."

I don't see how one can develop intellectually valid criticisms of any exiting situation when the information upon which these criticisms are based may not be valid in and of itself. Either the public health research community will confront problems within their own research with the same degree of energy and vigor which they use to confront arguments from pro-gun scholars or they won't.

NOTES

1. I exclude from the total number of gun injuries only suicides, which also may start off as being of interest both to medicine and law enforcement, but end up as being the only gun-injury events which do not share a provenance between those two groups.

2. Cf., D. Hemenway and D. Webster, eds., "Special Issue on the Epidemiology and Prevention of Gun Violence, Preventive Medicine, Vol. 79 (October, 2015) pp. 1 – 58.

3. Jens Ludwig and Phil Cook, Gun Violence, The Real Costs (New York, Oxford University press, 2002.)

59

4. C. Branas, et. al., "Academic Public Health and the Firearm Crisis: An Agenda for Action," American Journal of Public Health, Vol. 107, No. 3 (March, 2017), pp. 365-67.

5. Cf., https://wonder.cdc.gov/wonder/help/main.html#What%20is%20WONDER.

6. Cf., https://www.cdc.gov/nchs/icd/icd10cm.htm.

7. Cf., https://www.cdc.gov/ophss/csels/dsepd/ss1978/ss1978.pdf.

8. Excludes suicides and some number of self-inflicted, accidental injuries.

9. "Who Gets Murdered When Someone Uses A Gun?" https://papers.ssrn.com/sol3/papers.cfm?abstract_id=3171134.

10. https://www.thetrace.org/2016/01/gun-safety-standards/

11. https://www.cpsc.gov/s3fs-public/pdfs/blk_media_2000d015.pdf.

12. ibid., page 6.

13. https://www.cdc.gov/ncipc/wisqars/nonfatal/definitions.htm.

Study 4 – Where Are the Guns?

Ever since the Federal Government got into the regulation of civilian-owned firearms, the issue of where these guns are located and who owns them has loomed large. This is because guns are the one consumer product whose existence and use poses a threat to public safety; hence, placing controls around the product's availability has always been recognized as a government responsibility which can be carried out through regulations and laws. Even the vaunted 2008 Heller decision, which grants Constitutional protection to privet gun ownership also explicitly gives government the authority to determine who should and should not be able to have access to guns.[1]

Notwithstanding Heller, most states and many localities have also passed laws, and regulations covering access and use of guns, with the result that a small cottage industry has grown up in the gun violence prevention (GVP) research community that attempts to correlate the rate of gun violence with the number and comprehensiveness of gun laws.[2] One of the most comprehensive studies, conducted by a group of scholars connected to Boston's Children's Hospital and the Harvard School of Public Health, found that "a higher number of firearm laws in a state are associated with a lower rate of firearm fatalities in the state, overall and for suicides and homicides individually."[3] This finding and similar conclusions from other GVP-focused research has become a standard narrative to support the extension of gun-control laws at both the national and state levels.[4]

Trying to find a positive, inverse correlation between more gun laws and less gun violence, however, does not take into account what has been another significant finding by public health gun researchers, namely, the degree to which gun violence rates also correlate with the number of civilian-owned guns; i.e., more guns equals higher gun-violence rates. This finding first appeared around the time that the Federal Government enacted its first, comprehensive gun-control measure in 1968, and has been quantified and validated multiple times since that date.[5] Like the argument about more gun laws results in less gun violence, the connection between more guns and higher gun-violence rates has also become a standard narrative within the organizational GVP.[6.]

The problem with both of these arguments lies not in the assumption that gun laws and/or gun availability has no direct bearing on how and when guns are used. The real problem has to do with the fact that the data covering the number of gun laws and the rate of gun violence is captured on a state-by-state basis, yet nobody has been able to determine whether gun laws or gun-violence rates connect at all to the number of guns owned by civilians in each state.

Until and unless some method is developed to calculate the number of guns and gun owners on a state-by-state basis, comparing state levels of legal restrictions on gun ownership or gun violence rates to a global, national number of civilian-owned guns makes very little sense. It certainly can't take into account the degree to which guns, as opposed to other, regulated consumer products like cars, are not universally owned or used within the United States.

The most recent data we have on who owns guns and where these gun owners live is contained in the recent 'gun stock' survey conducted by researchers at Harvard and Northeastern Universities, which was an effort to update a previous survey published by Phil Cook and Jens Ludwig in 1994.[7] The updated survey queried 2,072 gun owners of whom 15% of lived in the Northeast, 23% lived in the Midwest, 37% lived in the South and 22% were residents in the West.

While these numbers support the generally-accepted notion of which regions contain a larger proportion of gun owners, as well as providing the membership backbone for the NRA, the lack of more specific, state-level data does not allow for measuring either the rate of gun violence or the impact of gun laws relative to the actual number of individuals with access to guns. In order to develop a valid statistical profile of where and how many guns exist in each state, we first have to explain how the supply-chain for this particular commodity is structured and works.

The Supply Chain.

As early as 1938, the Federal Government regarded the regulation of handguns as an important tool to aid law enforcement in their response to crime. This concept was embodied in the 1938 Federal Firearms Act (FFA38,) requiring all interstate shipments of handguns to be expedited only through licensed federal gun dealers, who could only transfer handguns to an individual who resided in the same state where the licensed dealers conducted his business. The requirement that interstate handgun traffic be managed through connections between federally-licensed gun dealers was extended to long guns (shotguns and rifles) in the 1968 Gun Control Act (GCA68) prompted by the interstate purchase of a Carcano 91/38 surplus rifle by Lee Harvey Oswald in March, 1963.

The federal firearms license (FFL) does not define whether the licensee actually engages in the buying or selling of guns; it simply is a record-keeping mechanism that allows the government to track the interstate movement of firearms, regardless of the reason why the particular weapon is moving from place to place. In 2015, the ATF listed slightly more than 56,000 active dealer licenses, all of whom can engage in the buying and selling of firearms, as well as slightly more than 8,000 pawnbroker licenses which can also be used by those establishment to buy, sell and receive or ship guns.

Since we are interested in determining how many guns are located in each state, we can ignore the inventories held by pawnbrokers because guns in their possession were previously shipped into the state for initial purchase from a gun dealer by someone who at some later date decided to pawn a particular gun. We can also ignore perhaps 2/3 of the individuals who are licensed dealers because that is roughly the percentage of FFL-holders who hold a license so they can take advantage of wholesale prices to buy personally-owned guns, but rarely engage in any significant amount of business-like transactions at all.

The estimate that two-thirds of FFL-holders are not involved in the supply chain which feeds the civilian arsenal is based on an analysis of the address of every FFL in the United States, with the state-by-state percentage of home-based licensees presented here:[8]

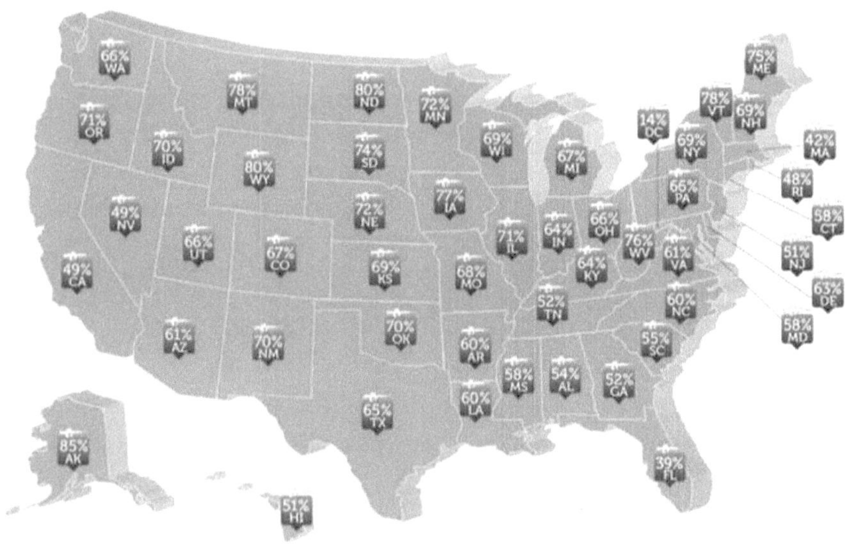

Note that very few states contain less than 50% home-based gun dealers, primarily because such states impose licensing requirements on gun dealers beyond the federal regulations, mainly not allowing for any kind of dealer activity unless it is carried out in a bricks-and-mortar storefront which meets appropriate zoning and police requirements in the jurisdiction where the dealer has a shop.

Of the 56,000 FFL dealers, probably less than 20,000 are actually in the business of selling guns to the public, and the number of federal licensees engaging in any degree of gun sales is probably half of that. For example, the ATF currently lists 365 licensed dealers in Connecticut, and assuming that 58% are home-based, this leaves slightly more than 150 who may actually be engaged in the business of buying and selling guns.

Smith & Wesson, which does a very aggressive job of enrolling retail gun shops in its dealer program, has only 25 brick-and-mortar stores listed on its website as being located in Connecticut, which is probably a fairly accurate number of the full-time gun shops operating in the state. Because Connecticut is in the Northeast where gun ownership is less common than in the South or the Midwest, we can expect to find a larger proportion of active, retail gun dealers in southern and midwestern states. I suspect that a solid figure for the number of gun dealers who earn a full or partial living from buying and selling guns in probably somewhere between 5,000 and 10,000, the latter probably too optimistic by half.

What is important to understand about the supply chain which links the producers of the product – gunmakers – to the consumer of the product is the fact that the major manufacturers (Glock, Sig, Smith & Wesson, Ruger, Taurus, Remington, Mossberg, Marlin) along with the second-tier and even smaller producers do not sell what they make directly to these retailers. For the most part, the total customer list for the gun makers consists of 30-odd national wholesalers, who compete between each other for business from the retail stores.

This two-tier distribution system used to be typical in most consumer products, but the advent of big-box, discount stores and chains has reduced wholesaling to a small fraction of the business it used to be. On the other hand, even though chain stores (Cabela's, Bass Pro) have moved very aggressively into gun retailing, I would probably be understating it if I were to say that 90% of all guns which enter the civilian arsenal probably first go across the counter of an independent, ma and pa store.

With the exception of Garen Wintemute's survey of gun dealers which queried 1,600 gun dealers who sold 50 guns or more each year, we have precious little objective data about how gun shops operate, particularly from a financial point of view.[9] Wintemute's survey calculated a median annual gun sale of 200 weapons, which in today's current market would bring in roughly $80,000 in gross sales. Since the revenue from gun sales represents somewhere between 80% and 90% of the total dollars which comes through a gun shop in an average year, it's clear that gun stores are hardly the type of business on which someone will get rich quick, or get rich at all.

The estimate of gross revenues derived by multiplying Wintemute's median of 200 gun sales by a per-gun average of current market values probably overstates retail gun dealer revenues because Wintemute did not ask his respondents to break down sales or inventory figures between guns that were new and guns that were used. The gun business is unique in the entire world of consumer products not just because of the licensing and regulatory requirements, but because the entire chain of commerce is based on products that never wear out.

Recall I mentioned above the 91/38 Carcano rifle purchased from a mail-order house in Chicago by Lee Harvey Oswald in 1963. This rifle was first produced in Italy in 1938, the specific gun shipped to Oswald was manufactured in 1940 and working models of this rifle can still be found and purchased in retail shops. For that matter, the inventories of many gun shops today include Moisin-Nagant military rifles which were manufactured for the Russian Tsarist government during World War I but were never shipped overseas because the Tsar disappeared in 1917.

In addition to the commerce in previously-owned firearms, which probably accounts for at least 30% of all guns transferred by retail dealers to customers, the other unique aspect of the gun industry supply chain is the degree to which the regulatory procedures embodied first in FFA38 and then expanded in GCA68 permits very little interstate movement of firearms beyond the initial state to which a new gun is shipped from wholesaler to retailer.

This last statement may appear to fly in the face of numerous studies concerning the illegal movement of guns from strong to weak regulatory environments, but notwithstanding the public and political concern about the scourge of gun 'trafficking,' the actual number of illegal gun transfers compared to the number of guns that remain within their initial state of receipt is scant.

In 2015, according to the New York State Attorney General, slightly more than 2,800 'crime' guns picked up in New York State had their origin in the neighboring state of Pennsylvania, the latter state being the third-highest 'iron pipeline' state whose guns ended up in New York.[10] That same year, at least 400,000 new handguns were received by retailers in Pennsylvania. If the number of guns that moved illegally from Pennsylvania to New York and other states was as many as 10,000, this would mean that the in-state gun stock would have been reduced by less than 3 percent.

In Chicago, a city that suffers from a disproportionate level of gun violence, the police recover roughly 7,000 'crime' guns each year, of which 20% flow over the border from gun shops in neighboring Indiana, where gun laws are weaker than in Illinois.[11] But each year gun dealers in Indiana add at least 150,000 new handguns to their inventories. Reducing the in-state gun stock by 1% of the new guns which flow into Indiana cannot be said to make a difference to the number of civilian guns within the Hoosier State.

The Data.

Since the Brady Law requires that dealers conduct background checks on every gun transferred from their inventories to a civilian purchaser, the background check numbers for each state gives us a fairly accurate view of where the guns go which are added to the civilian arsenal each year and the growth of that arsenal within each state. These numbers, however, must be used with caution for the following reason: The data published monthly on background checks does not differentiate between new versus used guns, which means that a certain proportion of all background checks cover guns that are already in the civilian arsenal. Since the background check data does not ask the retailer to differentiate new as opposed to pre-owned guns, the inventory disparity between these two categories cannot be measured using background check data or any other publicly available numbers.

The scholarship which uses ATF manufacture-import data to estimate the growth of the civilian gun arsenal may thus be overstating the annual growth of the civilian-owned gun stock by as much as 30 or 40 percent. This can be better understood by comparing ATF manufacture-import numbers to FBI-NICS checks.

In 2015 the number of manufactured and imported guns minus exports totaled 14,152,976. For 2014, the number was 12,559,905; for 2013, it was 14,076,939. Now let's compare these numbers to background checks for the same years.

	New Guns	Background Checks
2013	14,076,939	14,201,652
2014	12,559,905	12,543,131
2015	14,152,976	13,605,168

If every gun that was manufactured or imported each year ended up being transferred to a retail customer in that same year, the number of Brady background checks performed annually would give us a very precise measurement for the increase in the size of the civilian arsenal. But we cannot use any background check figure with this degree of precision, because we do not know the size of the unsold inventory held by wholesalers or retailers, and Wintemute's excellent dealer survey focused primarily on the regulatory, as opposed to the business side of retail gun activity.

.While we therefore cannot use background check data to develop a precise measurement of the civilian gun arsenal on a state-by-state basis, the data can certainly give us a very clear indication of the relative number of guns being introduced and circulated within each state, thus making it easier to determine the degree to which gun ownership must be considered as an important variable in comparisons of gun violence rates and the relative strength or weakness of gun laws.

Where the Guns Are.

While we cannot construct a definitive list of the number of guns existing in each state, the background check data does allow us to compare the degree of gun transfers on a state-by-state basis, which I believe to be a valid proxy for understanding the geography of the U.S. civilian gun arsenal. The Harvard-Northeastern gun-stock survey cited above found an increasing concentration of guns in fewer hands, if anything validating even further the use of NICS transfer data to understand the geographical dispersion of the civilian arsenal.

Based on a per-capita media transfer rate of 0.51 (calculated on the total of all transfers since 2001 divided by 2016 state population), we have placed all states into five quintiles, with the resultant numbers (red highest, black lowest) looking like this:

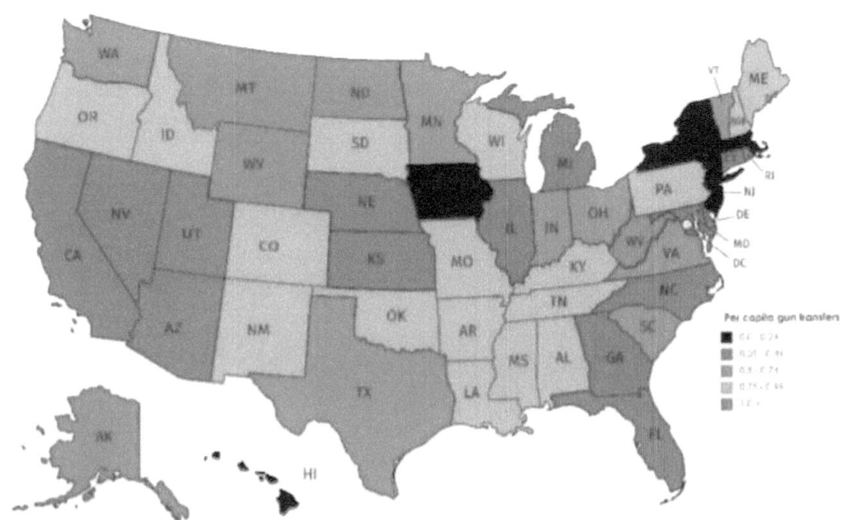

 The geographic dispersion of gun transfers differs from previously-published estimates of regional gun location in certain important respects. First, while some northeast states show the lowest per-capita rates of gun activity, note that certain southern states – North Carolina, Georgia, Florida – are also states with less than average gun transfers. This is a particularly surprising finding when we consider that Florida has always been considered the most pro-gun state in terms of serving as a legislative 'incubator' for laws making it easier for residents to gain access to guns. Florida was the first state in recent years to move from 'may' issue to 'shall' issue of concealed-carry permits and was also the state which passed the first stand-your-ground statute which then served as a model for similar statutes in other states.[12]

Using the data published by Fleegler (cf. footnote 3) I have constructed two maps, the first showing the degree to which each state has more or less gun statutes, or what Fleegler refers to as the legislative 'strength' of each state:

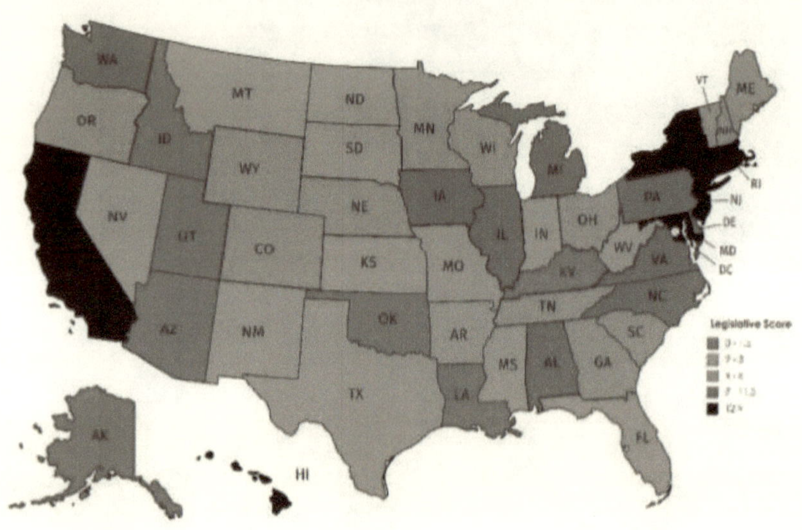

The second map shows gun-fatality rates on a state-by-state basis:

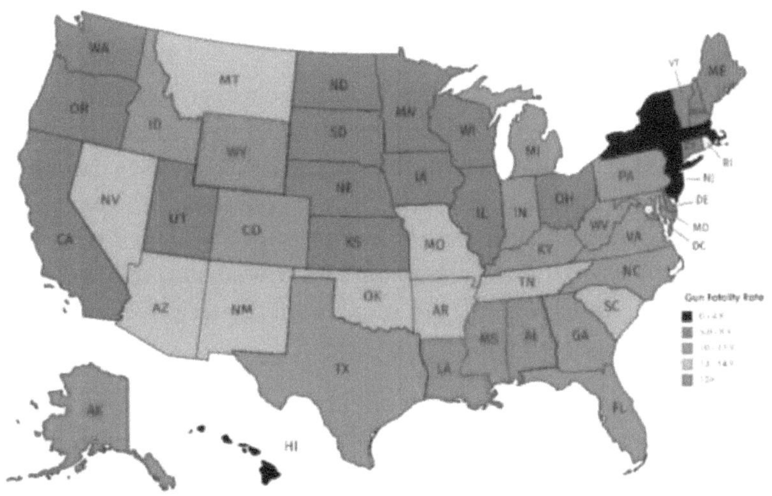

What emerges from the comparison of maps showing state-level rates of gun transfer activity, gun laws and gun fatalities is that the correlation between gun activity and gun fatality rates are just as positive or even more positive than the correlation between gun fatality rates and legislative strength. The only states which show a significant positive correlation between the lowest gun fatalities and strong legal environments are the urbanized, northeast states plus Hawaii, but these states also show the lowest rate of gun ownership using gun transfers as a proxy for ownership.

Once we move beyond the five or six most regulated states, which also happen to be the states with the lowest amount of gun transfers, any correlation between regulation and gun fatality rates becomes much less exact. If anything, a comparison of gun fatalities with state-level gun transfer activity appears to be more robust than comparing gun fatalities to the amount of regulations existing within individual states.

Further Thoughts

The purpose of this paper is not to undermine research which seeks to expand the gun regulatory environment by seeking connections between the incidence of gun violence and the degree to which laws can be used to regulate access to guns. Rather, this effort was designed to create a more nuanced argument about the path to reducing gun violence by considering how the overall level of gun activity and gun ownership might influence both the amount and scope of gun regulations, as well as the incidence of gun violence experienced within each state.

The fact that a state like Alabama would have a relatively strong legislative score while experiencing one of the highest gun mortality rates but also registering a high amount of gun transfers should alert us to the possibility that gun ownership may be as potent as gun-law strengths for explaining varying rates of gun violence from state to state.

Until and unless the government mandates a comprehensive background-check requirement for every transfer of a firearm, and also requires the background data to include information on new versus previously-owned guns, we cannot develop a reliable estimate for the growth of the civilian gun arsenal each year. On the other hand, the fact that gun violence rates at the state level appear to correlate more strongly with background checks, as opposed to legislative 'strengths,' should alert us to the possibility that any attempt to explain varying levels of gun violence from one region or state to another must take into account the number of guns present within each state, which may be a more important consideration than simply guessing at the percentage of gun owners in each state.

NOTES

1 https://www.law.cornell.edu/supct/pdf/07-290P.ZO, p.54.

2 E. Grinshteyn & D. Hemenway, "Violent Death Rates: The U.S. Compared with Other High-income OECD Countries," The American Journal of Medicine, 129 (2016), 266-273.

3 E. Fleegler, et.al., "Firearm Legislation and Firearm-Related Fatalities in the United States," JAMA Internal Medicine, Vol. 173, 9 (May 13, 2013) 732-740.

4 A summary of this argument, unfortunately without links to sources, can be found here: https://www.safehome.org/resources/gun-laws-and-deaths/.

5 G. Newton & F. Zimring, "Firearms and Violence in American Life," National Commission on the Causes and Prevention of Violence, Washington, D.C., Government Printing Office (1969).

6 Relevant statements on websites of all gun-control m=organizations, Everytown, Brady, etc. https://everytownresearch.org/gun-violence-by thenumbers/?source=etno_ETHomePage&utm_source=et_n_&utm_me dium=_o&utm_campaign= ETHomePage#America.

7 D. Azrael, et. al., "The Stock and Flow of U.S. Firearms: Results from the 2015 National Firearms Survey," Russell Sage Foundation Journal of the Social Sciences, Vol. 3, no. 5 (October, 2017) 38-57. The 1994 survey can be accessed here: P. Cook & J. Ludwig, "Guns in America: National Survey on Private Ownership and Use of Firearms," National Institute of Justice – Research in Brief (May, 1997) 1 – 12.

8 https://www.ffl123.com/ffl-dealers-per-state-by-population/.

9 G. Wintemute, "Firearms Licensee Characteristics Associated with Sales of Crime-Involved Firearms and Denied Sales: Findings from the Firearms Licensee Survey," The Russell Sage Foundation Journal of the Social Sciences Vol. 3, no. 5 (October, 2017) 58-74. Because Wintemute set his respondent criteria at annual gun sales of 50 or more, his findings are skewed towards larger dealers who account for a majority of aggregate gun

sales, but represent a much smaller proportion of all gun dealers engaged in actual gun commerce.

10 https://targettrafficking.ag.ny.gov/.

11 https://www.nbcchicago.com/blogs/ward-room/chicago-gun-trace-report-2017454016983.html.

12 Caroline Light, *Stand Your Ground: A History of America's Love Affair with Lethal Self Defense* (Boston; Beacon Press, 2017.)

Study 5 – Guns and Gun Violence.

What is the connection between the number of guns in private hands and the amount of violence caused by guns? Scholars have examined this question for more than forty years, and the consensus appears to be that the excessively-high rate of gun violence experienced in the United States is first and foremost caused by the excessively-high number of privately held arms.

This argument is based on comparing rates of violence between various countries, then comparing rates of fatal violence, then comparing per-capita rates of gun ownership. Regarding the initial comparison, the United States is no more violent than other advanced (OECD) countries. Even though definitions of culpable violence differ from one nation-state to another, the United States appears to fall somewhere in the middle of rates of intentional violence crimes for all the OECD states.[1]

When a comparison is made between fatal violence rates, however, the results dramatically change. The U.S. experiences three to seven times the rate of fatal violence found in other advanced nation-states. Here the comparisons are also a little less than ideal, because some jurisdictions count murder and manslaughter together as fatal violence, other penal-judicial systems count them as separate categories, but allowing for these differences in definition, the United States remains the murder capital for the entire OECD.[2]

When we then look at other, standard SES comparisons; i.e., income, employment, education, etc., none of these factors appear to play as salient a role as the degree to which Americans have access to guns and use these weapons to inflict most of the heightened level of homicides that occur within the United States. It should be noted that comparing the U.S. non-

78

gun homicide rate to what we find in other countries still has us sitting at the top of the heap. Thus, it would be more accurate to say that our access to small arms doesn't lift our fatal violence rate above everywhere else; rather, it takes a higher rate than what is experienced in other countries and makes it much worse.[3]

The relationship to gun access and intentional, fatal injuries in the U.S. versus other countries has been most recently discussed by Grinshteyn and Hemenway, in the 2015 article which updates earlier research published by Hemenway based on data through 2003, the 2015 piece bringing the argument forward with data through 2010.[4] In this respect, the argument connecting intentional gun homicide to the per capita number of guns follows from earlier work by Kellerman, Rivara and others linking increased levels of homicide and suicide to gun access within the civilian population.[5] Both arguments are compelling and have been accepted by virtually every advocacy organization trying to develop strategies to reduce violence caused by guns.[6]

There is only one problem with this universally-accepted explanation however, namely, that it fails to distinguish the types of guns which are owned by civilians versus the kinds of guns which are used to commit gun violence, either against oneself or against someone else. The fact that someone has a 'gun' in the home is not the same thing as the fact that they have a 'car' sitting in the driveway outside the home. Driving off in a car creates the same level of risk regardless of the type of car being driven away. Picking up a gun creates much different levels of risk depending on the type of gun.

The purpose of this article is to examine gun violence not from a quantitative point of view in terms of how many guns are used to commit injuries, but from a qualitative point of view, i.e., what types of guns are used to commit gun injuries. The importance of approaching gun violence from this perspective should not be underestimated because the regulatory system, developed in 1968 to reduce gun violence, presupposes that every type of gun should be regulated to the same degree and in the same way in terms of access and use.[7] But does such a blanket regulatory system reflect how different guns are used and therefore require the same degree of control?

The Data.

In fact, although there are endless studies on the number of guns that may or may not be owned by civilians, this data and the studies which utilize it do not go beyond distinguishing the gun stock beyond, at best, dividing all gun into two categories: hand guns and long guns, the latter being defined as any firearm with a barrel length of 16 inches or longer, obviously the former being defined as any firearm with a barrel of less than 16 inches in length. Where did this distinction come from? It was embodied in the first, federal gun-control law of 1934, and it is totally arbitrary in terms of what it says or doesn't say about different types of guns.[7] At best, it is a descriptive definition which tells us nothing about how a gun functions, or is used, or what it was designed to do.

Unfortunately, this broad and therefore basically useless definition of a 'gun' remains with us to the present day and is still the only descriptive used to define the American private gun stock from a qualitative point of view. Since 1968, every gun which enters the commercial gun market through purchase from s licensed dealer is designated either as a long gun or a hand gun on the ATF-devised registration form (4473) filled out at the point of transfer; the monthly numbers for each type collected and published by the FBI since 1999.[9]

Additionally, at the point of manufacture, when gun makers have to report the number of guns they produce upon which the payment of excise tax is based, they are required to break out the types of guns that leave their factories based on whether the gun is a pistol, revolver, rifle, shotgun, or semi-automatic weapon, as well as caliber.[10] But this information, which is aggregated and published yearly by the ATF, only speaks to the manufacturing of guns, not their ultimate movement into the civilian stock of guns.[11]

 The result is that we not only rely on estimates for how many guns are owned by Americans, we rely even more on estimates for how this gun stocks breaks down in qualitative terms. The most recent study claims that Americans today have an arsenal which is composed of the following gun types and percentages: pistols (26%), revolvers (12%), 'other' handguns (4%), rifles (33%), shotguns (20%) and 'other' guns (4%.)[12] The overall percentage of hand guns versus long guns is not substantially different from a previous survey conducted in 2004.[13]

 These survey estimates, however, tell us next to nothing about whether our current regulatory system is doing what it is supposed to do; namely, keeping guns from falling into the hands of people who will use them in inappropriate (self-harm) or illegal (assaultive) ways. In the case of self-harm, i.e., suicide, we have fairly reliable data on how many people intentionally kill themselves each year with guns, but we do not know to any specific degree what kinds of guns they use. As for gun assaults, we do not possess any reliable, published data on either what type of guns are used or how these guns may or may end up in unlawful hands. Even the degree to which gun violence defined as a criminal act is committed by individuals who are not lawfully allowed to own a gun is a subject which remains numerically undefined.

This paper breaks new ground in three respects. First, it is based on an analysis of guns used for intentional assaults, not just by type of weapon

81

(hand guns versus long guns which is the only defining category used by the FBI in their Uniform Crime Reports) but by caliber, manufacturer, gun model and age of gun. This analysis allows us, for the first time, to understand not just the relationship between guns and violence per se, but between different types of guns and gun violence.

Second, the paper also analyzes the types of guns utilized for suicide, again allowing us to understand this behavioral phenomenon from the perspective of the type of instrument utilized, rather than just the behavior and mental status of the victim.

Third, we also present details on the types, caliber and brand-name of stolen guns, again, data which has never previously been available within the public domain. What we learn from a specific analysis and comparison between these three 'crime gun' categories will then lead us to a more realistic view of the degree to which the current regulatory system can meet its intended goals.

The data for this study comes from police departments which collect, store and inventory all firearms received in the course of investigations for both criminal and self-injury events. It does not include guns that are received for reasons other than criminal investigations for injury (or threatened injury) such as guns that are abandoned or 'found,' or guns which are simply turned in by individuals who no longer feel the need to keep a gun in their homes. Many of these guns have been traced through the ATF National Tracing Center, but there is no requirement that any law-enforcement agency, other than federal agencies, are required to conduct a trace on any gun received. Some police departments conduct such traces, other agencies do not.

The jurisdictions whose data has been analyzed are Chicago IL, Baltimore MD, Denver CO, Sacramento CA and Chandler AZ. To maintain consistency, these five jurisdictions were examined for all guns collected and inventoried in 2014. The total guns studied for purposes of this article was 9,356, of which 8,714 were for legal violations involving guns, and another 642 were for guns recovered following suicides. Unfortunately, this disparity between crime guns and suicide guns does not reflect the degree to which two-thirds of fatal gun violence is driven by self-inflicted, fatal injuries.

On the other hand, our overall data is not just based on gun deaths, but aggregates all investigations involving the criminal use of a gun. Since such events (aggravated assaults, threats, armed robbery) easily exceed more than 200,000 on an annual basis, constructing an analysis of gun violence based on criminal gun use should show an overwhelming proportion of guns being used in interpersonal crime. The latest report from the National Crime Victimization Survey covering 2016, for example, shows that more than 480,000 people were victims of criminal gun use of one type or another.[14]

Suicide Guns

Insofar as our data sample for gun suicides is much more limited than the data we have analyzed for gun crimes, we begin first with a discussion about gun suicide. This section is based on suicide reports in 2014 from Denver, Baltimore, San Diego, Austin and Charlotte, for a total of 277 cases.[15] Of the other suicides contained in our overall data collection, the specific information on types of guns was not exact or complete enough to be used for understanding the types of guns chosen for a suicide event.

In these five cities, we were to identify specific guns in 233 cases. We divided the guns into four categories: new hand guns, old hand guns, new long guns and old long guns. We classified a hand gun as new if it was sold on the commercial market any time after 1980; an old hand gun was any hand gun that was not sold on the commercial market after 1980,

although such guns could be purchased as used guns from a licensed
dealer. We followed the same designations in the case of long guns.

In 2014, of the five states whose data was used for this part of the study,
only Maryland required registration of private hand gun transfers beyond
the initial sale by dealer to consumer. This requirement did not apply to
long gun transfers and there was not any registration requirement for hand
gun transfers in the other four states. The Maryland registration
requirement may explain why only Baltimore had a 50-50 division between
hand guns and long guns used for suicide. Totals for all five cities are
presented here:

	OH	NH	OL	NL	
Austin		13	4	2	
Baltimore	10	18	20	7	
Charlotte	25	35	28	1	
Denver	3	19	8	1	
San Diego	4	26	7	2	
Totals	42	111	67	13	233

(Key = OH and OL are handguns and long guns manufactured prior to 1980;
NH and NL are handguns and long guns manufactured since 1980.

 Note that of the 233 suicide guns, two-thirds (n=153) were hand guns. Of
these guns, nearly three-quarters were 'new' hand guns; i.e., they might
have been purchased from a dealer either new or used. The 42 'old'
handguns would probably have been transferred privately or were
purchased prior to the registration requirements of GCA68. As for the

long guns, they were overwhelmingly pre-1980 models, and of the 80 total long guns, most were either military surplus weapons or obsolescent shotguns. Of the new long guns, we could only identify 3 guns that would be considered modern hunting weapons.

In terms of understanding access to weapons by individuals who use guns to commit suicide, this data has certain limitations. Most important, it covers guns recovered by police agencies operating in major, urban centers, whereas suicide is much more a function of small towns and rural populations. In those latter jurisdictions, we would expect to find a much larger proportion of long guns as being connected to suicide events, particularly in western and mountain states like Montana and Idaho whose suicide rates are far above national levels.

On the other hand, this data reveals and substantiates the idea that placing greater restrictions on hand gun purchases, particularly licensing requirements such as permit-to-purchase (that decreases the speed with which a hand gun can be acquired) may play a positive role in reducing gun suicide. The fact that only the city of Baltimore had an almost equal use of hand guns and long guns may support this hypothesis, but it doesn't necessarily mean that the suicide rate in Baltimore was less than it would have been if city residents had unlicensed access to hand guns through private sales.

Crime Guns.

The data on gun crimes comes from two sources. One source is a listing of 846,353 guns inventoried by 1,054 law enforcement agencies in 36 states and Washington, D.C. between 2010 and 2016, and published by *The Trace*. Suicide data analyzed above comes from the same dataset. The other source, again published in *The Trace,* is a detailed dataset covering all 'crime guns' picked up by the Chicago P.D. over the course of 2014.[16]   Of the total numbers, more than 90% were guns picked up by agencies investigating a crime to which the particular weapon was connected, or in police parlance, 'recovered.' The remaining guns were either reported as stolen or came into agency possession for some administrative reason not directly connected to a specific crime.

The data analyzed for this section of the article only covered 'recovered' guns; i.e., guns used in specific crimes; we will analyze stolen guns in the following section We did not break down gun types by crime categories because those listing were created at the time the gun was seized and could not reflect the ultimate disposition of any particular criminal case. Nevertheless, virtually every gun recovered by an agency during a criminal investigation was connected to a serious crime. The important exception in this respect were guns listed in inventories as being seized for a firearm 'violation,' i.e., illegal possession of a gun which may or may not have been connected to another, specific crime. Such guns represented roughly 20% of all inventoried weapons.

 The crime guns that we specifically identified as to name, date of manufacture, type, model and caliber, were the 7,926 recovered in Chicago, Baltimore and St. Louis over the course of 2014. In that year, these three cities represented and still represent major concentrations of gun violence, with Chicago registering a per-100K murder rate of 15, Baltimore at 34 and St. Louis at 50. The 2014 national rate was 4.98.[17]

Not surprising, when we compute the number of crime guns relative to the overall size of each city's population, an interesting correlation appears. The number of crime guns recovered in each city was:

Chicago   3,160

Baltimore   1,876

St. Louis   1,539.

But when we compute crime guns per-100,000k population, the numbers look like this:

St. Louis   487

Baltimore   301

Chicago   166

Now look at the per-100,000k murder rate for each city:

St. Louis   50

Baltimore   34

Chicago   15

In other words, as the murder rate in a particular jurisdiction goes up, so does the rate of crime guns recovered by the police. Which means that the more guns floating around, the more guns become the method of choice for ending someone else's life. This is a very important finding because it introduces a significant nuance into the usual argument about more guns equals more criminal violence. The nuance is as follows – more guns equals more gun violence in a particular jurisdiction perhaps depending on how many guns can be accessed in one place as opposed to another.

Of the total 7,926 crime guns recovered in these three cities, 5606 (70%) were center-fire handguns, of which 3,408 were guns commonly found in retail gun shops, the brand breakdown looking like this:

87

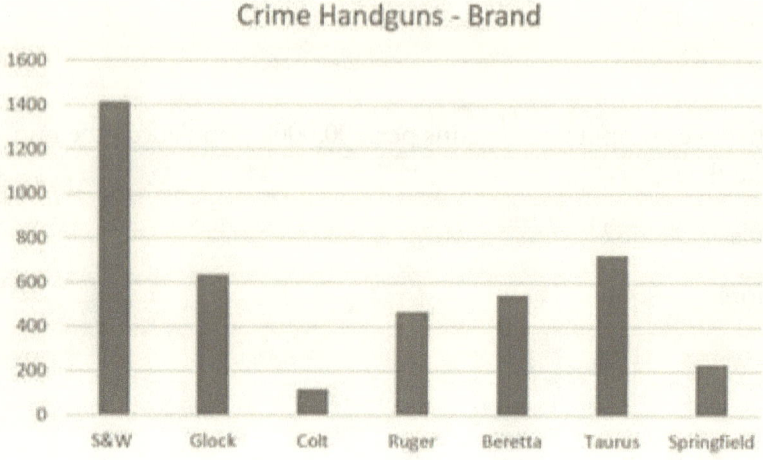

Of the remaining 2,300 handguns, 1,376 would have to be classified as old, used junk, with the traditional, racially-tinged 'Saturday-night Special' sobriquet applying to most of these guns. The junk guns included nearly 700 RG-Rohm guns which used to be imported from Germany but stopped coming into the U.S. following the import prohibitions imposed by GCA68. The continued distribution of these 'junk' guns then shifted to domestic manufacture, a story partially explained by Wintemute in a study covering some of these companies which operated (and still operate) in California.[18]

The fact that nearly one-quarter of all recovered crime handguns were manufactured either by foreign or domestic gun makers, most of whom ceased operations more than twenty if not thirty years ago, should alert us to a second, very important finding that emerges from the data under review. While the lack of serial numbers for all recovered guns from Chicago (most of the St. Louis and Baltimore guns did include serial numbers) makes it impossible to determine, with any degree of accuracy, the average age of every crime gun, it is possible to estimate the date of manufacture through an analysis of the type and model name of each gun.

The issue of date of manufacture is of primary concern to gun regulators and gun-control advocates because a significant amount of gun regulation activity involves tracing of crime guns and the development of what regulators call 'time to crime,' or TTC. The TTC numeric is used by law enforcement to identify both individuals and gun dealers which show up more than an average amount as the sources of guns whose TTC is brief. It is assumed that any gun connected to a crime that was initially brought into the commercial market in less than two years may be a gun whose initial transfer was a 'straw' sale; i.e., it was purchased for the express purpose of being resold and thus moved from legal to illegal hands.

According to the most recent TTC report issued by the ATF, the average TTC time for 141,476 guns traced in 2016 was roughly ten years, for our three states it was twelve years for Maryland, nine years for Illinois and six years for Missouri.[19] There are two problems with this data, of which the ATF appears to be unaware of both.

First, the TTC number is calculated by determining the amount of time which has passed from the first date a gun was sold by a dealer to the date that the ATF received a trace request. But for at least 40% of all guns, which is the average percentage of used guns found in retail gun shops, the first transfer date cannot be used to figure out when a particular gun began the movement from legal to illegal hands. This time-span can only be figured out if the specific trace started on the date that the gun was last sold in a retail shop. In other words, the overall TTC average is probably longer than it should be for at least 40 percent of all traced guns.

Second, what comes out from the Baltimore-Chicago-St. Louis crime gun list is the fact that it is impossible to determine the initial date of manufacture or sale of at least one-quarter of all the guns connected to

89

criminal investigations in those jurisdictions; one would probably find this percentage to be constant in every police jurisdiction within the United States. This is because the same cheap, older guns not only appear with the same degree of frequency in all three cities whose crime guns we analyzed in detail but are also found in virtually every other jurisdiction that we sampled in order to validate the overall results.

Some of the older guns which appeared in police inventories have not been manufactured for a century or more. For example, Mossberg manufactured a 4-shot derringer called the Brownie, from 1920 to 1932. More than 40 of these guns turned up in the crime gun listings in Baltimore, Chicago and St. Louis (most of them in Chicago) but we found them in other cities as well. Both Colt and Browning manufactured 25-caliber 'baby' pistols, the former first appearing in 1908, the latter in 1906. The Colt guns were serialized right from the first guns, but the Browning guns didn't get serialized in any organized fashion until 1954. Both of these guns appeared in all of our police lists.

While centerfire pistols were 70% of all crime guns in the Baltimore-Chicago-St. Louis lists (and were roughly a similar proportion in other jurisdictions that were sampled) the remaining 30% were divided roughly in half between 22-caliber guns and long guns; i.e., rifles and shotguns. In the rifle category, less than 2% of all recovered guns were assault rifles (AR and AK) and the only hunting rifles were a handful (6) of lever-action guns in 30-30 caliber. There were virtually no bolt-action or semi-automatic hunting rifles recovered in any of those cities, and even in more rural Western jurisdictions such as cities in Colorado, hunting and sporting guns accounted for less than 2% of all crime weapons.

In addition to understanding what types of weapons account for gun violence, we also need to look at the ammunition which accounts for deaths and injuries from guns. Somewhat arbitrarily, we have decided that crime guns which cause gun violence are those weapons chambered for

90

any center-fire round. The reason for this is because the rim-fire cartridge family (22 short and 22 long rifle) do not show up in great numbers in counts for gun injuries, nor are they prevalent in the types of ammunition carried in the crime guns picked up by Chicago P.D.

The most popular street caliber was 9mm, which comprised 25% (n=1,037) of the 4,113 calibers identified in the 2014 list of crime guns. The next most common caliber was 38 Special with 10.7% (n=443) 10of all identified calibers, followed by 40 S & W, which was 10.6% (n=438) of all crime guns. A total breakdown of all handgun calibers looks like this:

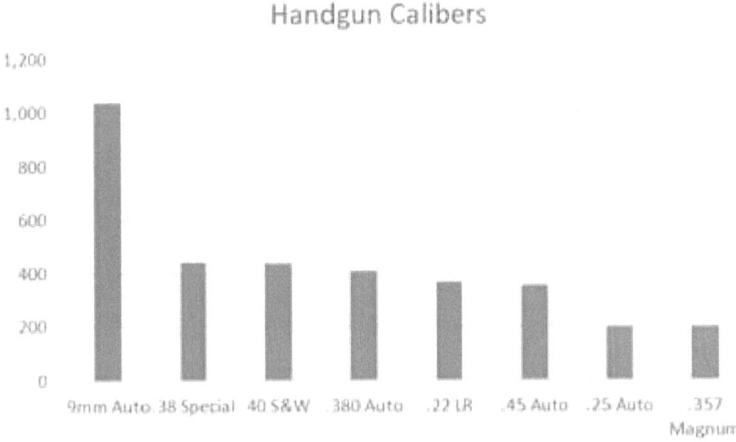

Of the remaining 655 identified calibers, a few additional handgun calibers show up (44 Magnum, 45 Long Colt) of which 40% were shotgun calibers and 60% were 22 calibers, but half of the latter came from guns that were either no longer manufacture or more than thirty years old.

Data from the National Violent Death Survey confirms the degree to which gun violence is basically a function of centerfire ammunition.[20] For 2015, the percentages of gun deaths from each caliber were as follows:

9mm	31.1%
22 cal.	8.7
357	3.6
38	6.1
40 S&W	16.8
45	10.4
25 – 32	8.2

This adds up to 80% of all bullet wounds, the total percentages from assault-rifle categories was 2.2% and hunting calibers represented exactly two bullets out of 2,118 identified rounds, the latter also possibly assault rifle rounds.[21] In other words, ammunition calibers associated with crime guns validates that most gun violence is committed with guns that fire centerfire, handgun ammunition.

Stolen Guns.

For this section of the report, we rely on the 651 stolen guns reported to the St. Louis Police Department in 2014. It should be noted that while we have estimates that somewhere between 200,000 and 400,000 guns are stolen from privately-held locations each year, these numbers are based on public opinion surveys, they do not represent any hard data at all.[22] This is because: a) very few jurisdictions require that civilians report stolen guns to the police; and b) we assume that many guns are stolen from individuals who are not legally allowed access to guns in the first place.

The latter issue about stolen gun data, namely, the illegal ownership of guns, imposes severe limitations on making any definitive judgements about the quantity or types of stolen guns. There is probably not a single law enforcement agency in the entire United States that will enter information on a stolen gun without receiving and validating the name and address of the individual who calls in the report. Which means that probably a majority of guns stolen every year remain totally outside the purview of the law, nor will the estimates on gun thefts, all of which come from public surveys, include thefts of 'illegal' guns as well.

That being said, an analysis of the guns reported stolen in St. Louis in 2014, still gives us some important information about the types of guns which end up contributing to gun violence and violent crime. Of the 466 handguns whose calibers were identified in the report, the breakdown of specific calibers was as follows:

Caliber	Number	Percent
22-	25	0.055
38	118	0.259
32	6	0.013
357	10	0.022
9mm	169	0.371
45	47	0.103
25	5	0.011
40S&W	76	0.167

Note that the percentages of guns stolen on a caliber basis conforms to calibers identified as being the most frequently used in gun crimes: 9mm, 38 and 40 S&W. This breakdown of stolen gun calibers compared to gun-crime calibers is also similar to what was found for both assault rifles and shotguns, because neither category registered more than five percent of all stolen guns, with assault rifles accounting for 4% and shotguns accounting for 5% of stolen calibers, respectively. Furthermore, of all the guns reported stolen, only 12% were long guns of any type, the other 88% were classified as handguns, with pistols accounting for more than 80% of all handguns stolen in 2014.

As for older guns, only 17 specific junk guns were found on this list, of which half were made by Jimenez Arms, the remainder being Davis, Bryco and the ubiquitous RG. But we suspect that the percentage of the older guns would have been significantly higher were it not for the fact that of the total number of 561 stolen guns, 153 were reported without any brand identification at all. More than 90% of the unidentified guns by brand name were classified as handguns, leading us to believe that many of them might have been older guns as well, an assumption not completely supported by the data at hand.

Not surprisingly, of the handguns which could be identified by manufacturer, the most common brands were Smith & Wesson, Taurus, Ruger and Glock, together accounting for 52% of all handguns on the stolen list. Again, this data corresponds to what we found for the percentage of commonly-owned handguns connected to gun crimes.

Summary

Putting all the data together, we arrive at the following conclusions about guns that are used in every type of gun violence – intentional injury against oneself or someone else. This paper does not contain any data on unintentional gun injury, first because gun accidents are not considered to be any kind of violence; second, because the number of unintentional fatal and non-fatal shootings (approximately 17,000 each year) can hardly be considered a serious health issue, given the existence of more than 300 million guns in private hands.

If the data presented above tells us anything about the connection between guns and gun violence, it is that this entire discussion should be revised to focus not on the number of guns in the civilian arsenal, now estimated between 265 million and 395 million, but should focus on the number of handguns owned legally and illegally by Americans. Putting together the three categories that we have examined – suicide, crime, theft – centerfire handguns account for 70 percent of guns in all three categories, with the percentage of centerfire handguns in the crime gun category rising to 80 percent.

 Do we have a gun violence problem in this country because we own so many guns? What we actually experience is a gun violence problem because we own centerfire handguns, which is a much more exceptional situation in comparative, global terms, than the overall size of the civilian arsenal itself. If we could gather reliable data on handgun ownership within other advanced countries, we would probably find that the per capita comparisons currently made between the size of the U.S. civilian arsenal to the size arsenals in other countries would be dwarfed by when comparing only the number of handguns that are privately owned.

The reason we need to focus more directly on handgun regulation, as opposed to regulating guns in a generic sense, is that the only way we can craft effective and meaningful regulatory policies is if our regulatory strategies aim (pardon the pun) not at solving the problem of gun violence in a generic sense, but the violence caused by the misuse of handguns. Because we do not focus on regulating the guns which cause gun violence,

95

we are spending time, energy, physical and financial resources on
regulatory procedures which cannot reduce gun violence at all.

The five rifles above (top to bottom) are the Remington 700, the Ruger
77, the Winchester 70, the Marlin 1894 and the Savage 11. Together, these
guns represent at least 40 million of the total number of guns owned by

Americans today, which is somewhere between 10% and 15% of the entire pile of guns that exists throughout the United States. How many of these five models were found in a word-search of the 846,353 guns inventoried by 1,054 agencies throughout the United States? Exactly five.

It may be the case that a specific word search did not pick up every, single instance in which one of those guns was listed as a stolen, criminal or suicide gun by the police. Cops are human, they make mistakes, and as our analysis on St. Louis stolen guns makes clear, perhaps as many as 20% of all the stolen guns listed in the national inventory could not be identified as to which company manufactured the gun. But if any of those models had constituted even a fraction of the guns analyzed for this effort, the examination we conducted on thousands of the guns would have brought such weapons to light.

In addition to guns that virtually never contribute to gun violence for reasons having to do with model and types, there is also the issue of using regulatory procedures which cannot begin to yield any information which would aid law enforcement agencies in understanding how a particular gun ended up in the 'wrong' hands. Our detailed analysis of crime guns in Baltimore, Chicago and St. Louis clearly indicates that at least one-third of all guns connected to criminal violence cannot be traced beyond the individual who used the gun to commit a particular crime. Either the guns were manufactured by gun makers who went out of business prior to GCA68, or they were imported before GCA68, or they were manufactured before the law required serialization of all small arms.

In fact, even the ATF admits that although they processed 408,000 traces in 2017, they were only able to correctly identify the type of gun and its first place of sale in less than 325,000 trace requests, a failure rate of 20 percent.[26] Recall that we described 'junk' guns as representing perhaps as many as one-third of all crime guns recovered each year. The ATF trace data confirms the degree to which old, untraceable handguns circulate in large numbers throughout every jurisdiction within the United States.

Much of the reluctance on the part of gun-control researchers and advocates to avoid pursuing strategies that would restrict handgun ownership is based on the idea that the 2008 Heller decision giving Constitutional protection to guns commonly found in the home takes a handgun ban, de facto or de jure, off the table.[27] Thus, avoiding the policy implications of what this paper demonstrates not about gun violence, but about handgun violence, continues to be an issue that gun-control advocates go out of their way to avoid.

Even though perhaps as much as 40 percent of all civilian-owned guns are handguns, a careful reading of Scalia's majority opinion in Heller, along with an understanding of handgun function and design renders the 2nd Amendment argument not just inappropriate but completely wrong. Scalia differentiates between weapons that are 'commonly owned,' as opposed to 'unusual' weapons; i.e., military weapons or what we usually refer to as weapons of war. And basically what he is arguing is that someone who keeps a Glock or a Sig in their house for personal defense wouldn't take this weapon with them if they were called up to serve.

What Scalia didn't understand, nor did anyone else on the Court have a clue, was that virtually all the handguns which are used to commit gun violence happen to be designed for military use and are carried by troops in every battle zone today. The current pistol used by the U.S. Army is a Sig whose design is incorporated into every handgun manufactured in the SigArms factory and sold to military and civilians worldwide. Gaston Glock developed his first gun (and every subsequent model is designed in exactly the same way) in response to an Austrian Army RFP. That we have decided, for purely political reasons, to allow gun makers and gun importers to sell weapons of war to the general public doesn't change the fact that not just the assault rifles, but virtually all the handguns now 'in common use' (to quote Scalia) do not possess any intrinsic 2nd-Amendment protection at all.

This is the reason why any discussion about gun violence is at best incomplete, at worst simply wrong, if the discussion does not contain clear references and understanding not just to the perpetrators and victims of gun violence, but to the types of guns used to commit this kind of violence every day. If it were the case that crime guns represented a random assortment of all the guns held by civilians, then we would have no choice but to continue building and refurbishing a regulatory system that attempts to impose the same restrictions on every type of gun and every individual who owns any type of gun.

This paper clearly demonstrates that the individuals who commit gun violence are making very conscious and deliberate choices about what kinds of guns they should use, and what types of guns won't meet their requirements for the violence they choose to impose. If our aim is to reduce gun violence, knowing the guns is an important aspect of understanding how and why the violence occurs.

NOTES

1. https://www.worldlifeexpectancy.com/cause-of-death/violence/by-country/.

2. http://www.unodc.org/unodc/en/data-and-analysis/crime-and-criminal-justice.html.

3. M. Weisser, "Is Gun Violence an Example of American Exceptionalism?" https://papers.ssrn.com/sol3/papers.cfm?abstract_id=3158214.

4. E. Grinshteyn & D. Hemenway, "Violent Death Rates: The U.S. Compared with Other High-Income Countries, 2010," The American Journal of Medicine, 129 (2016) 266-273.

5. A. Kellerman, F. Rivara, et. al., "Gun Ownership as a Risk Factor for Homicide in the Home," New England Journal of Medicine, 329 (1993), 1084-1091; Kellerman & Rivara, et. al., "Suicide in the Home in Relation to Gun Ownership," NEJM, 327 (1992), 467-472.

6. Cf., website content from Brady, Everytown, etc.

7. The qualifying information required by a prospective gun owner prior to purchasing a legal small arm can be found in the ATF 4473 background-check form, in particular Questions 11a – 11i. https://www.atf.gov/firearms/docs/4473-part-1-firearms-transaction-record-overcounter-atf-form-53009/download. This qualifying information is the same for all legal firearms transferred from a licensed dealer to a gun purchaser.

8. https://www.atf.gov/rules-and-regulations/national-firearms-act.

9. https://www.fbi.gov/file-repository/nics_firearm_checks__month_year_by_state_type.pdf/view.

10. The annual manufacturing report can be accessed here: https://www.atf.gov/about/docs/undefined/afmer2016webreport508pdf/download.

11. The annual firearms commerce report can be accessed here: https://www.atf.gov/news/pr/atf-releases-2017-report-firearms-commerce-us. It does not give any data on the locations to which imported or manufactured firearms are shipped for consumer resale.

12. D. Azrael, et. al., "The Stock and Flow of U.S. Firearms: Results from the 2015 National Firearms Survey," The Russell Sage Foundation Journal

of the Social Sciences, 3, 5 (October, 2017).
https://www.rsfjournal.org/doi/full/10.7758/RSF.2017.3.5.02.

13. Hepburn, L., et. al., "The U.S. Gun Stock: Results from the 2004 National Firearms Survey," Injury Prevention, 13, 1 (2007), 15 – 19. DOI: 10.1136/ip.2006.013607.

14. Rachel E. Morgan, Ph.D., and Grace Kena, "Criminal Victimization, 2016," U.S. Department of Justice, Office of Justice Programs, (December, 2017), p. 5.

15. The information on suicides comes from the dataset that can be downloaded from The Trace (https://www.thetrace.org/missing-pieces-data/) which was collected and analyzed by Daniel Nass and Bryan Freskos. We discuss the dataset in the Crime Guns section.

16. https://www.thetrace.org/2016/01/chicago-crime-guns-raw-data/.

17. National murder rate from CDC-WISQARS. City rates from local media reports on murder numbers announced by law enforcement, then factored against U.S. Census population estimates.

18. G. Wintemute, "Ring of Fire - The handgun makers of Southern California : a report from the Violence Prevention Research Program," (Santa Barbara, 1994.)

19. https://www.atf.gov/news/pr/atf-releases-2017-us-firearms-trace-data-report.

20. We wish to thank Catherine Barber of the Harvard University School of Public Health Injury Control Research Center for this data.

21. Frank Zimring, "The Medium is the Message: Firearm Caliber as a Determinant of Death from Assault," I. J. Legal Studies, 97 (1972) 97 –

123, who found that half of the 1970 fatal shootings in Chicago were committed with gun chambered for either 22 or 25-caliber ammunition.

22.https://www.americanprogress.org/issues/gunscrime/reports/2017/07/25/436533/stolenguns-america/.

23. In 2016, according to the CDC, there were 58,854 unintentional deaths, the largest category for all deaths in that age cohort. Of these deaths, 234 were from firearm injuries; i.e., .003%.

Study 6 – Regulating Guns.

The Federal Government got into gun control big time in 1934, with the passage of the National Firearms Act, usually referred to as the NFA. This law created a list of weapons that were considered too lethal to be allowed into civilian hands unless the would-be owner submitted to a very detailed background check and paid a tax for each NFA weapon which would be worth more than $4,000 today.[1] Chief among the NFA weapons were full-automatic guns, also known as 'tommy guns,' of the type used by the Al Capone gang at the St. Valentine's Day massacre in 1929.

A second federal gun-control law was passed in 1938 which regulated both the commerce of guns as well as their ownership and use. As to the former, the 1938 statute required that anyone engaged in the buying and selling of small arms, a.k.a., a dealer, had to register with the federal government, purchase a federal firearms license, (FFL) and maintain records covering the sale of guns. As to the latter, ownership of small arms, the 1938 law, known as the Federal Firearms Act (FFA) for the first time defined certain types of individuals, particularly felons, who could not own or purchase guns.

The shift away from regulating guns based on a weapon's lethality and towards regulating guns based on the behavior of the gun owner came full circle with the passage of the 1968 Gun Control Act (GCA68.) This law enumerated nearly a dozen 'prohibited categories' and proscribed gun ownership or purchase for anyone whose behavior placed them into any of those categories, such as being convicted or charged with a violent crime, licked up in a mental hospital, hooked on drugs – this list of prohibited behaviors being expanded from time to time.[2]

Had federal gun laws after NFA continued to focus on product lethality rather than on user behavior, there is a good chance that today's current level of gun violence would not exist. The initial draft of the NFA proposed that handguns be included on the list of prohibited guns, but the final draft of the law saw this issue rubbed out. On the other hand, until the early 1960s, most Americans believed that handguns should not be legal for ownership or use except by law enforcement and qualified, armed guards.[3] Access to handguns is what distinguishes the U.S. gun culture from every other advanced national state, a distinction that goes hand in hand with a U.S. gun-violence rate that is 7 to 20 times higher than any other member-state in the OECD.[4]

The current gun debate, which escalated to a new level after Sandy Hook and took on an even greater dimension following Parkland, basically divides into two, well-defined groups. On the one hand, there are many national and local organizations demanding more laws and restrictions both on gun-owner behavior (e.g., comprehensive background checks) and gun design (e.g., assault weapons ban); on the other hand, there are national and local organizations which want a strengthening or extension of what is referred to as 2nd-Amendment 'rights,' or a lessening of restrictions both on gun-owner behavior (e.g., concealed-carry outside the home) and gun design (e.g., reducing the number of items on the NFA list.)[5]

Although there has been no substantive change in federal gun laws since 1994, one year after the Newtown massacre, The New York Times calculated that 109 new laws had been passed in various states, of which laws which loosened restrictions on gun ownership exceeded laws which tightened restrictions by a margin of two to one.[6] More recently, the Giffords Law Center, a prominent gun-control group, states that this 2 : 1 margin has remained constant from 2013 through the beginning of 2018.

While state-level legislation appears to favor the proponents of gun 'rights' over the proponents of greater gun restrictions, public opinion surveys from Gallup, Pew Research and the public health gun-research group at Johns Hopkins University all show that significant majorities of both gun-owning and non-gun owning Americans believe that more, not less restrictions should be placed on the ownership, use and design of guns:

- The most recent Gallup poll taken in 2018, found that 67% favored stricter laws covering the sale of firearms, the highest rate since 1993;
- A Pew Research survey in 2017 found that more than 75% of gun owners favored expanding background checks beyond the initial point-of-sale;
- A just-released survey from the Center for Gun Policy and Research at the Bloomberg School of Public Health extended the percentage of gun owners who supported expanding background checks to more than 85 percent.

The Problem.

How is it that the consensus between gun owner and non-gun owners on the need for greater gun restrictions continues to build in favor of tighter laws, yet at both the federal and state levels such laws fail again and again? There have been exceptions to the inability of gun-control advocates to mount serious challenges to the power and sway of gun-rights groups, the most notable being the recent legislation in Florida, a.k.a., the 'gunshine state,' which passed a post-Parkland statute reinstating a three-day waiting period for gun purchases, but also granted school officials the right to arm teachers, thus eliminating educational locations as gun-free zones.[7]

This remarkable case of cognitive dissonance between how Americans allegedly view gun regulations and the degree to which such regulatory initiatives fail to get enacted into law is usually ascribed to the power and authority of something called the 'gun lobby,' which purports to be highly-organized political movement supporting gun 'rights.' The movement is led, so it is claimed, by the National Rifle Association (NRA,) whose three, or four or five million members (depending on which estimate you choose to believe) are quick and eager to bang the drums whenever a state legislative committee considers a gun bill either pro or con.

There are two problems, however, with picturing the NRA as the Grand Wizard behind every nefarious attempt to loosen gun rights. First, the degree to which legislators are beholden to the NRA's financial 'clout' is overstated, because at the national level, the average Member of Congress can count on receiving, at best, less than 3% of what is needed to finance an electoral campaign from the Fairfax group.[8] Much more important, however, is the fact that the so-called 'nationally representative' surveys showing agreement between gun owners and non-gun owners regarding certain gun regulatory strategies fail to take into account or even mention specific gun strategies which are specific to the narratives and outlooks of the two sides.

For example, the 2014 Pew survey in 2014, 'Priorities for Gun Policy,' listed ten strategies, of which only one (arming school personnel) is backed by gun-rights groups.[9] The Giffords Center has published an extensive guide to what they refer to as polling results for "commonsense safety," again restricting the list of polls to strategies that gun-control organizations support, with or without any degree of consensus from the other side.[10]

The most singularly detailed survey on attitudes about gun regulations comes out of the Johns Hopkins gun-research group, whose 'nationally representative' survey conducted by the NORC's AmeriSpeaks organization, which claims to be a 'breakthrough panel-based research platform,'[11] consists of yes-no answers to 24 regulatory policy ideas, of which 23 ideas reflect the agendas and perspectives of gun-control groups.[12] Like the Pew surveys, the Hopkins study also divides respondents into gun owning and non-gun owning groups, with the latter invariably supporting every proposal to a greater degree than the former, although a majority of gun owners also evidently support two-thirds of the entire proposal list.

Let me make it clear again that I am not questioning the validity, the
assumptions or the agenda of any of the organizations and research
groups which conduct such surveys in the hopes of developing a
consensus between gun owners and non-gun owners over public policies
that might reduce the 125,000 deaths and injuries from guns that we suffer
each year, a number which seems once again to be climbing over the past
several years. What I am questioning, however, is the construction and
results of national surveys whose definitions of both 'representative'
survey panels and 'commonsense' or 'reasonable' gun regulations, I believe
to be flawed. Let's speak to the panel issue first.

The Hopkins study (and the Pew surveys) ask respondents to identify
themselves as gun owners or not. In other surveys, a differentiation is
made between gun owners and people who are household members where
guns are located but aren't the owners themselves. Creating a panel based
on gun ownership assumes that: a) gun owners are willing, ready and able
to disclose their gun-owning status to a survey as easily and/or frequently
as individuals who don't own guns. And while legal gun ownership has
become more mainline as state after state adopts more liberal licensing
policies on concealed-carry (CCW) of guns, the most recent estimates on
the issuance of CCW sets the national number at somewhere around 15
million, which represents less than 20% of the adults who either own guns
or live in gun-bearing homes.[13] The gap between overall gun-owning
numbers and the number of individuals who allow law enforcement
agencies to keep a record of their ownership status certainly creates the
possibility that the accuracy of any 'nationally-representative' panel
comprising gun owners may be tentative at best.

Creating a survey about guns, then asking respondents to identify
themselves as gun owners also creates issues of bias and responsiveness
depending on which organization conducts the survey itself. The average
gun owner is an older, white male who lives in a small or medium-sized
town in the South or the Midwest, votes Republican, describes himself as
politically conservative and has a post-high school education usually

108

consisting of technical training at a community college or vocational school. How do you think someone with such a background is going to feel when he is asked about guns from someone connected to the University of Chicago or the Bloomberg School of Public Health?

In addition to the representativeness of the panels themselves, a bigger problem arises when we look at the list of policies created by the Hopkins group which gun owners and non-gun owners are asked to review and state whether they support such policies or not. The Hopkins survey lists 24 policy initiatives, of which only one, allowing guns to be brought into K-12 schools, is endorsed by any of the major pro-gun organizations, and even the vaunted extension of background checks to secondary transfers and sales, which both Pew and Hopkins find substantial support from gun owners, has been openly denounced by the NRA.[14]

This is not to say that the gun-rights coalition is bereft of ideas for how to reduce violence caused by guns. To the contrary, the NRA, NSSF and other pro-gun organizations have long endorsed a wide planch of strategies to keep America safe from gun violence, most of their ideas focusing on the positive social utility of owning and carrying a gun. On April 29, 1992 a television news team in a helicopter filmed and transmitted a video of a group of Black youths attacking a white truck driver, who made the mistake of driving through the middle of Los Angeles during the first night of the riots which erupted after 4 cops were found innocent of beating up Rodney King. The next day, there wasn't a gun shop in America that didn't sell out all its self-defense guns, and while serious and valid public health research began to validate the idea that guns were not so much a benefit as a risk, this scholarship could not and did not alter the attitudes of many Americans who increasingly believed that safety from crime and violence was best assured with access to a gun.

In 1959, a Gallup poll asked a cross-section of Americans how they felt about a ban on civilian ownership of all handguns, and 60% supported the idea. In 1993, the first time that Gallup ran this same survey after the riots surrounding Rodney King, support for a handgun ban had fallen to 42%.

The percentage of gun-ban supporters would never again rise above 40%, and now sits at 28% in the survey dated October 5-11, 2017. Since most surveys which put the percentage of gun owners at or below 40%, obviously many of the respondents to the gun-ban poll are people who do not necessarily own guns.

To clarify where America really stands on gun control strategies, the survey I conducted does not divide respondents into two opposing camps and then asks them to state their opinions only on strategies promoted by one side. Rather, this survey is based on answers from 1,557 respondents whose demographics meet standard representative census criteria for gender, age, location and income, regardless of ownership or non - ownership of guns. The problem with trying to create a representative survey panel based on gun ownership status is that this criterion happens to vary significantly from state to state and sometimes vary even more significantly within individual states.

In addition to grouping all respondents regardless of gun-owning status, this survey breaks new ground by asking how respondents feel about 12 different strategies for what is referred to as 'gun-control' laws, with 6 laws representing strategies advanced by gun-control organizations versus 6 laws promoted by the other side; i.e., the gun-rights folks. According to *Survey Monkey*, the survey has a margin of error of less than 3% and has been validated for statistical significance (I'll spare the reader the usual verbiage boiler-plate in this respect.) The survey ran from May 24 through June 3, 2018.

The Survey.

Here is the demographic breakdown of respondents. Total respondents – 1,558. We begin with gender, the question answered by 1,547, of which

2%, not shown below, said their gender was something other than female or male:

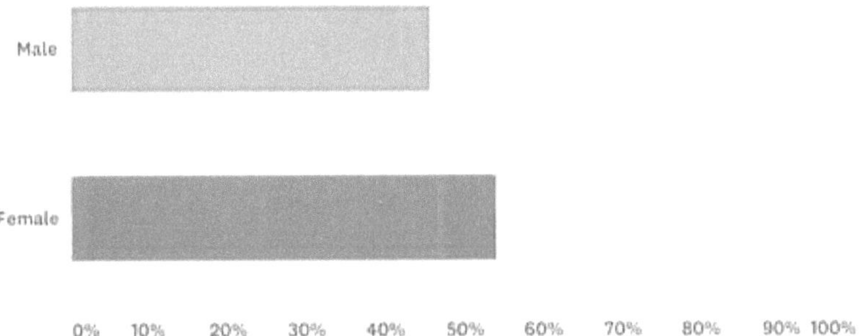

The age of respondents, a question answered by 1,557 respondents, the question for which an answer was required to submit a completed survey:

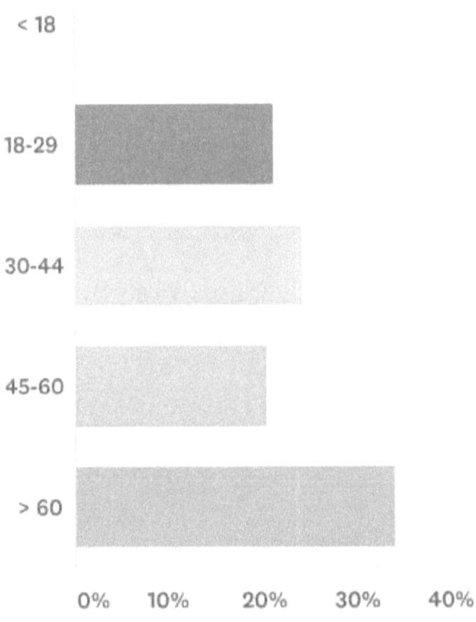

The household income of respondents, this question answered by 1,227:

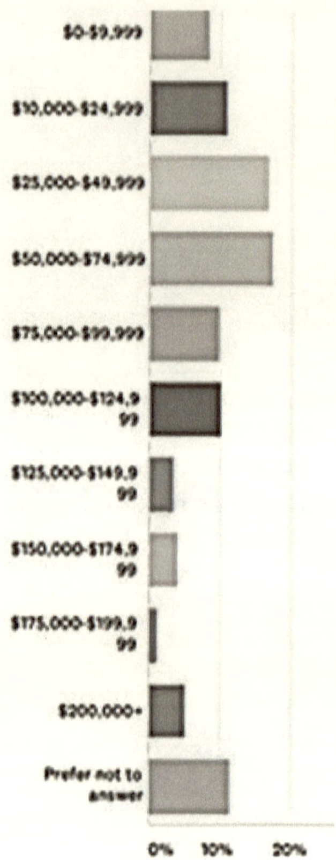

The residence by census area, answered by 1,208:

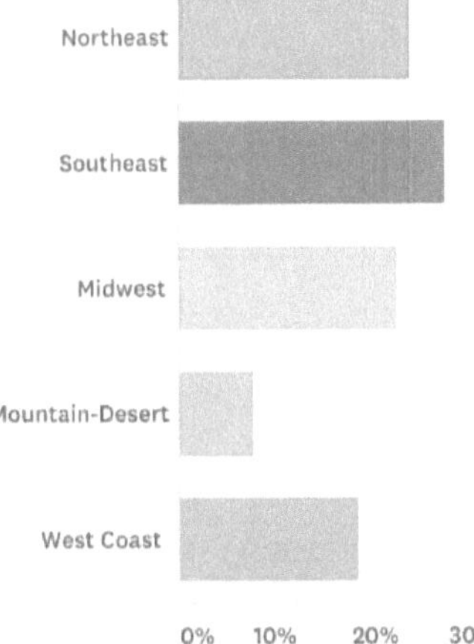

The breakdown for every one of these categories conforms to census data, the one exception being the age cohorts where this census has respondents above age 60 as 35%, whereas the current census 60+ age cohort is slightly above 20%. This difference will be adjusted when I filter the answers to specific questions about gun laws against respondent age. Note that 11% of respondents did not submit an answer about household income, which nevertheless did not basically change the distribution of income cohorts for the survey.

Respondents to the survey were asked their opinion on 12 specific gun-laws initiatives, 6 of which are being promoted by gun-control advocates, the other 6 by gun-rights groups. Here are the questions broken down by gun-control versus gun-rights categories.

<u>Gun-Control Questions</u>:

1. Are you in favor of background checks for all gun transfers? (Q2)
2. Do you support a ban on assault-style rifles like the AR-15? (Q4)

3.   Do you support a ban on gun magazines that hold more than 10 rounds? (Q6)
4.   Do you think that gun owners should be required to keep all guns locked or locked away at all times? (Q8)
5.   Should everyone be required to pass a proficiency/safety test before owning a gun? (Q10)
6.   Should handgun purchases require additional licensing beyond the FBI-NICS background check conducted by a dealer? (Q12)

None of these questions were skipped by more than 10 respondents. At the very least, this implies a near-universal understanding of the question's content itself. These questions were chosen because they are not only found in the published advocacy agendas of virtually every gun-control organization, but they also form the substantive basis for proposed legislation at both the federal and state levels.

Note that the texts of Q8 and Q10 include the word 'required.' This is a very important code-word in both gun-control and gun-rights camps because it means some degree of formal, governmental intervention in the procedures covered by both questions, and it is the role of government which most acutely divides the two sides in defining their basic approach to gun ownership.

<u>Gun-Rights Questions</u>.

1.   Are you in favor of eliminating gun-free zones so that people can protect themselves? (Q1)
2.   Do you support concealed-carry without special licensing so that all gun owners can choose whether they want to protect themselves with a gun? (Q3)
3.   Do you believe that if someone has a concealed-carry license from one state that he/she should be able to travel to any state with a concealed gun? (Q5)

4. Do you believe that everyone who commits a crime with a gun should serve a mandatory prison sentence? (Q7)
5. Should people be allowed to own handguns after age 18? (Q9)
6. Should gun safety be taught in K-12 schools? (Q11)

These questions represent policies which have been the most frequently-promoted legal strategies of the gun-rights movement, both at state and national levels. Q5 – national concealed-carry, is virtually several Senate votes away from becoming national law, having been introduced in every Congressional session since 1997. Eliminating gun-free zones is a current talking-point of President Trump and handing out 'tough' prison sentences for gun crimes is now SOP of the Justice Department under Jeff Sessions. Hence, like the questions representing gun-control strategies, these gun-rights questions are also part of the ongoing, public debate about guns. None of these questions were skipped by more than 10 respondents.

If the Pew and Hopkins surveys are correct, we should find some degree of support for the gun-control initiatives from the gun-owning population, which we have set at 44%. In other words, what we are looking for in Questions 2, 4, 6, 8, 10 and 12 is support whose floor would be higher than 56%; i.e., all the non-gun owning population plus some of the gun owners. Here are the percentages of support for all questions reflecting gun-control strategies for curbing gun violence:

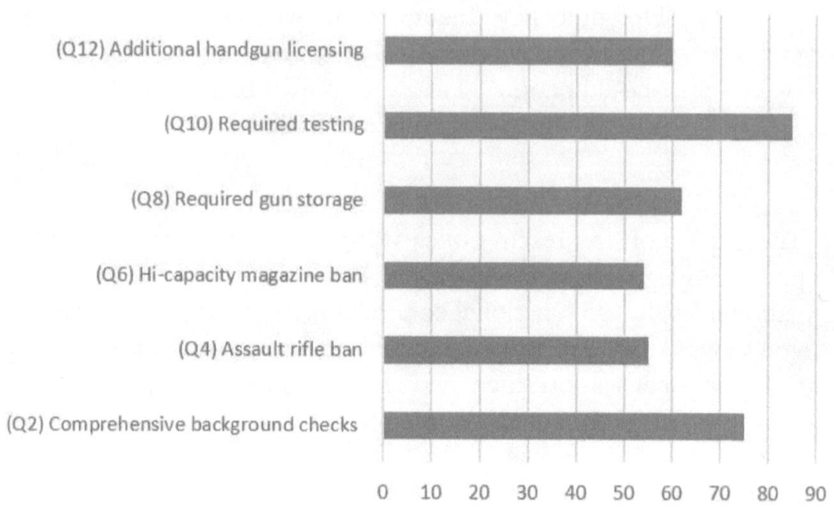

Note that four of the six gun-control strategies did not receive support (<4% margin of error) beyond what would have been registered if we assume that 40% of the respondents to this survey were gun owners and would therefore not support initiatives developed by advocates for gun control. I am surprised somewhat at the degree of support for Q10 – required testing – and I am not sure that using the word 'required' for this question was necessarily understood to mean government intervention in the process. The response to Q2 also has some nuances which will be explained in the Appendix following this text.

Now we need to examine the answers to Questions 1, 3, 5, 7, 9 and 11 which form the basic gun-law strategies for gun-rights advocates and groups. If any of the answers to these questions received more than 40%, we will assume that the overall percentage included both all gun owners and non-gun owners as well.

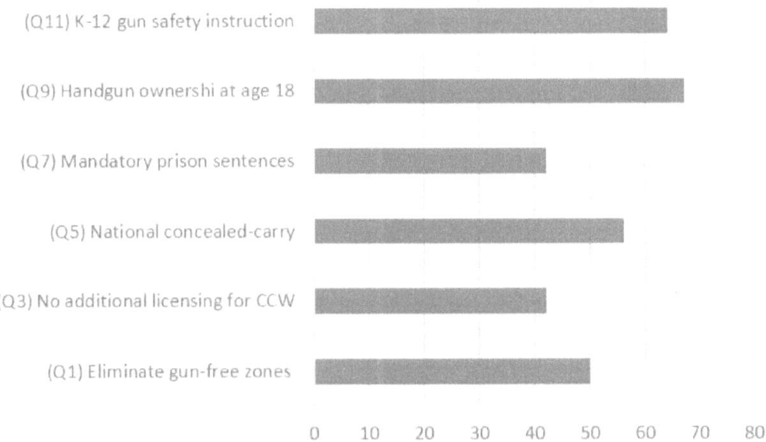

Four of the six questions representing public policies advocated by gun owners and pro-gun organizations received responses more than the percentage of respondents who would be identified as gun owners in any of the 'nationally representative' surveys. In other words, there appears to be more cross-over from the non-gun owning population than the other way around. Again, several of these questions gave respondents more options than just answering with a simple 'yes' or 'no,' an issue of nuance that will be discussed in the Appendix that follows the main body of the text.

Now let's cross-tabulate the questions based on specific demographics, staring with Q1, gun-free zones. This question asks respondents whether they support the abolition of gun-free zones, which has been a significant demand of the gun-rights movement and has been a basic pro-gun argument made by Trump both before and after the 2016 vote. Almost half the male respondents (48.8%) said 'yes,' negatives for this position were 29.8%. Respondents could also give a more detailed reply, stating that they favored eliminating gun-free zones except in K-12 schools (4.5%) or positive unless for the presence of armed guards (8.4%) or 'not sure' (6.9%.) Women on the other hand, only supported eliminating gun-

117

free zones to 26.7% and were opposed in 44.1% of their responses. Women expressed a much higher degree of doubt about the issue (15.5%) but supported retention of K-12 gun-free zones to the same degree as did the men.

Where we find the most significant cross-tabulated differences in the entire survey is in the comparison of responses by gender based on whether the questions reflected a pro-gun or a gun-control point of view. For every one of the 6 questions which represent a gun-rights priority, males responded more positively than females, from a difference of 5% for Q7 (mandatory prison sentences for gun crimes) to a difference of nearly 50% for Q1 (eliminating gun-free zones) and Q2 (universal background checks.) Conversely, women more strongly favored every gun-control initiative, with gaps of 50% for Q4 (assault-rifle ban) and Q6 (hi-cap magazine ban.) On average, women gave all six gun-rights initiatives 46.5% of their support; women gave gun-control initiatives 79% of their support. In other words, when the gun-rights movement speaks, it is largely speaking to and for men; when the gun-control movement speaks, it is basically reflecting a female view about guns. This should come as no surprise, given that men probably represent 85% of the owners of America's private stock of guns.

Perhaps the most interesting overall result in the survey was the difference between support for pro-gun laws (national RTC, eliminating gun-free zones, etc.) versus the degree of support registered for gun-control laws (comprehensive background checks, assault-weapon ban, etc.) Of the 6 questions covering pro-gun laws, Question #3, allowing for RTC without special licensing, was approved by 693 respondents, disapproved by 851. It was the only question in the entire that registered more negative than positive responses, and the gap (more than 20%) was substantial. Although the other 5 pro-gun questions all scored more positives than negatives (4,267 positive, 2,627 negative), add in the responses to Question #3 and the overall support for pro-gun laws was 55%. Only Question #9 (handgun ownership at age 18) and Question #11 (K-12 gun safety instruction registered support higher than 55%, in both cases roughly 66%.

On the other hand, for the laws that reflected gun-control strategies, the overall support for all 6 laws was 66%, and support for comprehensive background checks (Question #2) and required proficiency/safety course prior to gun ownership (Question #10) were 85% and 80% respectively. It should be noted that 5 of the questions, in addition to answer options consisting of 'yes' or 'no,' also gave respondents additional options. An analysis of these more detailed responses is found in the Appendix.

Conclusions

By eliminating the gun-owner versus non-gun owner from the identity of respondents and giving all respondents an opportunity to express their views on laws that reflect both sides in the gun debate, I believe we have created a survey which, for the first time, presents a clear picture of how Americans feel about regulating guns. And not surprisingly, what emerges from this survey is the idea that laws which reflect the gun-control agenda are supported by a greater margin than laws which reflect 2nd-Amendment 'rights.'

On the other hand, and this is a very important finding, every one of the pro-gun legal options gained a higher level of support than what represents the percentage of gun-owners in the general population. We will look at several of these responses in more detail in the Appendix, but in crafting legal strategies, the gun-control community should know while every gun-control legal option gained substantial support well beyond a simple majority, there were also pro-gun legal options which clearly generate support beyond gun owners themselves.

Here is a comparison of percentages registered for gun-control laws (Q's 2, 4, 6, 8, 10, 12) versus gun-rights laws (Q's 1, 3, 5. 7, 9, 11):

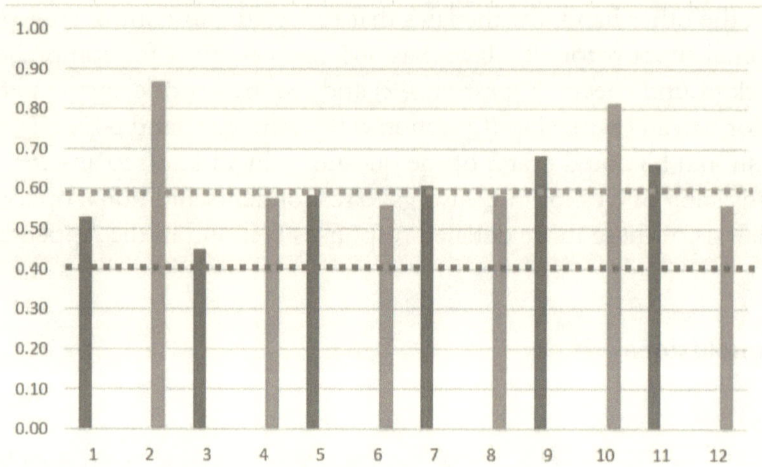

Note that only 2 of 6 laws favored by the gun-control community registered support above the benchmark level of 60%, which might indicate that these measures also would be supported by some gun owners. In contrast, every one of the measures advanced by the gun-rights community also received some degree of support from non-gun owners, if 40% is a valid fault-line for the number of Americans who own guns. While Questions 2 (comprehensive background checks) and 10 (required proficiency/safety training) received support well above the 60% line, which means that these issues were also receiving support from gun owners, no other gun-control legal proposal even reached a 60% rate. On the other hand, every gun-rights legal initiative received more than a 40% approval rate, with Q9 (dropping minimum age for handgun ownership to 18) and Q11 (teaching gun safety in K -12 schools) receiving nearly 70% support, which means that it is considered positively by almost as many non-gun owners as gun owners.

Aggregating all gun-control questions takes us to an overall approval rate of 66%, which mean that a slight number of gun owners also favor certain gun-control policies. But the overall approval rate for gun-rights initiatives was 59%, meaning that the gun provisions favored by gun-rights advocates received as much as three times more support from non-gun owners as gun-control initiatives received from the gun-owning population.

Again and again I hear gun-control advocates lamenting the fact that they cannot seem to find a 'middle ground' with gun owners in which discussions about 'reasonable' gun regulations can take place, hopefully leading to 'sensible' strategies for reducing gun violence. This survey clearly demonstrates that some gun owners will consider supporting regulations like comprehensive background checks and pre-ownership proficiency testing. At the same time, legal initiatives favored by the gun-owning community are attracting substantial support from the other side. Why should the ideas favored by gun owners be considered any less reasonable than the laws which gun-control advocates want to enact?

Appendix

Of the 12 questions contained in the survey, 5 questions gave respondents an opportunity to choose a somewhat more nuanced answer than simply opting for a 'yes' or a 'no.' The other optional answers were not included in our analysis of how gun owners and non-gun owners viewed gun laws in an overall sense, the complete response list for these questions clearly demonstrates that these issues are considered in some degree of detail by many Americans. (Slight overcount because of rounding.)

Q1. Are you in favor of eliminating gun-free zones so that people can protect themselves?

- Yes   40%
- Yes, except for K-12 schools
  5%
- Yes, unless there is armed security
  8%
- No
  35%
- Not sure
  11%

Q2. Are you in favor of background checks for all gun transfers?

- Yes
  72%
- Yes, but only for handgun transfers
  3%
- Yes, but not for transfers between family members
  10%
- No except for dealer sales
  11%
- No background checks on any sales
  4%

Q4. Do you support a ban on assault weapons like the AR-15?

- Yes
  52%
- Yes, but grandfather in existing guns.
  11%

- No
  38%

Q6. Do you support a ban on gun magazines that hold more than 10 rounds?

- Yes
  51%
- Yes, but grandfather in existing magazines.
  10%
- No
  40%

Q7. Do you think that someone who commits a gun crime should receive a mandatory sentence?

- Yes
  42%
- Yes, but judges should have sentencing discretion
  31%
- No. Depends on the circumstances.
  27%

NOTES

1.Calculated in value of 2015 dollars. See: https://data.bls.gov/cgi-bin/cpicalc.pl.

2.Current prohibited categories are found on the FBI-NCS background check form: https://www.atf.gov/firearms/docs/4473-part-1-firearms-transaction-record-over-counter-atf-form-53009/download.

3. Cf., Gallup poll: http://news.gallup.com/poll/1645/guns.aspx.

4. E. Grinshtyen & D. Hemenway, "Violent Death Rates: The U.S. Compared to Other High-Income OECD Countries, 2010," American Journal of Medicine, 129, 3 (March, 2016), pp. 266-73.

5. Reducing the number of NFA-regulated products is behind the campaign by Donald Trump, Jr., to promote the sale of gun silencers: https://www.thedailybeast.com/how-donald-trump-jr-helped-push-the-now-highly-controversial-gun-silencer-bill.

6.https://archive.nytimes.com/www.nytimes.com/interactive/2013/12/10/us/state-gun-laws-enacted-in-the-year-since-newtown.html.

7. https://www.nytimes.com/2018/03/08/us/florida-gun-bill.html.

8.https://www.opensecrets.org/orgs/recips.php?id=D000000082&type=P&state=&sort=A&cycle=2016.

9. http://www.pewresearch.org/topics/gun-control/2014/.

10. https://giffords.org/learn/.

11. http://www.norc.org/Research/Capabilities/Pages/amerispeak.aspx.

12. https://ajph.aphapublications.org/doi/full/10.2105/AJPH.2018.304432.

13. https://crimeresearch.org/2016/07/new-study-14-5-million-concealed-handgun-permits-last-year-saw-largest-increase-ever-number-permits/.

14. From the NRA: "NRA opposes expanding firearm background check systems, because background checks don't stop criminals from getting firearms, because some proposals to do so would deprive individuals of due process of law, and because NRA opposes firearm registration." Cf., https://www.nraila.org/get-the-facts/background-checks-nics/.

Study 7 - John Lott.

Not everyone hates John Lott. I am told that his cats like him and he evidently gets along well with his wife. But in the world in which he has been circulating for the past twenty-odd years, the people who consider his writing about gun violence positively are outweighed by the critics perhaps by a ratio of ten to one. You would think that at a certain point his critics would tire of making the same criticisms about him which they have been making since he published in 1997 his initial argument about guns and crime. But the fact that he continues to find both verbal and written editorial space in the public domain somehow provokes his critics to keep responding in kind.

I am going to argue in this paper that much of the criticism of his work is badly misplaced and owes more to the shortcomings of how the gun-violence prevention (GVP) community approaches the issues which continue to elude any objective attempt to derive effective public policies from the direction and shape of GVP research. Let me make it clear that I am not, *pace* public statements about me to the contrary, either an apologist for, or a research partner of John Lott. In fact, along with subjecting the work of his critics to a well-deserved, critical review, I also intend to state my own issues with John's thesis that more guns equal less crime.

At the same time, I do not believe that anything is gained by continuing the silly, rancorous and self-fulfilling attacks on his work because: a) the fact that his argument has launched him into public prominence as a representative of the pro-gun lobby does not, in and of itself, convey any special meaning regarding the value of his work; and b) such tactics obscure what is the important issue which still remains to be understood; namely, whether gun ownership is a benefit or a risk.

The issue of benefits versus risks of guns has been the central dividing-point between the pro-gun and anti-gun advocacy groups since 'gun control' became a flash-point for political debates in the 1980's and 1990's. On the one hand, America has a distinctive gun 'culture' which has played out over the decades because of the cowboy legends, as well as free access to hunting lands, both examples of a national exceptionalism not found in any other Western national-state. On the other hand, this culture, coupled with the existence of a civilian arsenal which numbers in the hundreds of millions of guns, also results in deaths and injuries from guns in numbers far above what is found anywhere else.

The risks versus benefits argument of gun ownership thus places gun injuries on one side of the equation as opposed to guns as protective devices on the other side. This is the debate to which Lott's book, *More Guns, Less Crime (MGLC)* marks a fundamental contribution which argues for the benefits of gun ownership as outweighing the risks. And because the book is a serious, detailed work, it has been used again and again by pro-gun advocates to bolster their case.

Had Lott simply published his book, then sat on the sidelines and moved onto something else, he would not be the *bête noir* of the gun-control community that he has come to be. This can be best understood by comparing the tone and content of two critiques of his work, written by the same authors, the first which appeared in 1999 prior to the publication of *MGLC*, the second which appeared in 2003 following the publication of *MGLC*.[1] The 1999 paper begins with a very polite comment about Lott's willingness to share the data he used for his research and goes on to raise substantive but not overwhelming criticisms in a scholarly way; the 2003 paper goes to great lengths to show Lott's affinity for promoting his views in public and media venues and then states as its objective to prove that what Lott argues is false. I am going to look at both papers in detail below, but I do find it interesting and somewhat ironic that John Donohue would take umbrage at Lott's conscious attempts to inject

127

himself into the public domain when Donohue would join with Steven Levitt in 2001 to publish the single most inflammatory, racist and disgusting social science research ever to appear, an article which Levitt then used as the launching-pad for the most egregious, self-promotion campaign ever concocted by any member of academe.[2] Be that as it may, let's return to Lott.

Because John Lott has become something of a fixture on pro-gun media channels and occasional op-ed space in various online and print venues, the gun-control advocacy community never misses an opportunity to remind its constituency that he represents everything about America's fixation on guns which many members of this community both fear and resent. The fact that his work has also been loudly scored and dismissed by various academic researchers whose work promotes various strategies to reduce gun violence, adds to the cacophony of anti-Lott responses whenever and wherever his name appears. For example, although a panel of criminologists convened by the National Research Council in 2005 could not state definitively whether Lott's work either proved nor disproved his thesis about more guns leading to less crime, gun-control scholars like Donohue used the panel's lack of any final validity-determination to declare that his research had been "definitively rejected," a judgement which is simply not true.[3] Back to Lott.

Lost in the arguments back and forth about whether guns are good or bad, what Lott's work represents is yet another contribution to an even wider and more compelling debate involving the decline of violent crime which occurred throughout the United States beginning in the mid-1980's, cresting in the early 1990's, and in certain localities going back to levels last experienced in the 1970's or even before.[4] In 2015, the Brennan Center for Justice at NYU's Law School published a comprehensive study that tried to evaluate the impact of 13 'popular theories' on why crime declined by more than 50% since 1991, noting that many of the theories had been the subject of previous research.[4] The end notes to this study contained hundreds of references to publications which directly or indirectly referenced this issue; in other words, conducting research on the 'great crime decline' has been a veritable cottage industry for various social science disciplines over the last twenty years.

I find it interesting that not one of Lott's critics has ever mentioned his work in the context of understanding how and why violent crime has followed such a unique trajectory since the early 1990's, even though this issue forms the very first words of the 1st edition of Lott's book: "Does allowing people to own or carry guns deter violent crime?"[5] And while the book contains more than 100 charts, graphs and other econometric and public survey data, the attempt by his critics to respond by putting forth their own charts, graphs and econometric modeling equations simply obscures what is basically a very simple and logical argument which is totally and completely ignored.

When Lott first began researching this issue several years prior to the publication of initial findings in 1997, crime rates were beginning to come down, but America's belief that a gun could serve as a deterrent to violent crime was going up.[6] In 1959, the Gallup organization asked Americans how they felt about a ban on private handgun ownership and 60% of the survey respondents thought it was a promising idea. By the time Lott published his article which found an inverse relationship between gun ownership and crime rates, percentage support for a handgun ban had fallen to the mid-30's, sitting in the low 20's today.

One of the initial criticisms of Lott's work was a paper by Tim Lambert, an Australian researcher whose 2004 attack on Lott continues to be cited as a fundamental rejection of the thesis that more guns equals less crime.[7] Lambert's paper states that Lott has created a cause and effect argument based on the idea there are more guns, that there is less crime, the former therefore causes the latter. He then says that for this argument to be true, that all three parts of the argument must be true. Unfortunately for Lott, the initial proposition according to Lambert, is not true.

129

Lambert claims that over the period covered by Lott's research (1977 – 1992) that there weren't 'significantly' more guns. He bases this statement on a combination of public surveys and some piecemeal manufacturing data, accusing Lott of only referencing several surveys which appear to indicate a per-capita increase in the number of people who own guns. Lambert cites the existence of 86-gun surveys since 1959, citing as his source a book by the criminologist and pro-gun researcher, Gary Kleck[8]. Had Lambert consulted Kleck's earlier work, *Point Blank: Guns and Violence in America*, he would have found more accurate data on the growth of the American civilian gun arsenal that would have shown that Lott's argument about the increase in gun ownership was correct.

The most accurate way to determine gun ownership is to look at the data published by the ATF on the number of guns manufactured each year because small arms are not the type of item to accumulate in substantial numbers on gun maker's inventory shelves. If a certain gun maker, let's sat Smith & Wesson, produces half a million guns in a year, the chances are that all those guns will have been shipped to wholesale outlets within a few months after the next year begins. In 2016, Smith & Wesson registered $722 million in annual sales, the year-end value of its inventory was $74 million; i.e., 10% of what was produced and sold.

The ATF numbers show an average increase in yearly gun production of roughly 2% beginning in 1988 and continuing up to the present time. More important has been the increase in handgun manufacturing, not only on a year-to-year basis within that specific product category, but as a proportion of all guns being produced each year. In 1970, handguns accounted for 26% of the entire civilian gun stock. By 1980 handguns were 30% of the total, which rose to 33% by 1987. In 2000, the handgun percentage of all guns was 35%, rising to 36% by 2007. By 2008 and for every year thereafter, for the first time since the Gary Kleck and then the ATF began keeping track of annual firearm production, handguns exceeded the production of long guns every year.[9]

That Lambert does not understand either how to access production data nor make a distinction between hand guns and all privately-owned guns renders his ability to analyze anything having to do with American gun violence rather moot. Americans didn't begin applying for RTC licenses, nor did they pressure state governments to make RTC issuance more flexible because they wanted to go out and buy a long gun. The fact that gun production shifted from long guns to handguns while RTC licensing spread from a handful of jurisdictions to just about every state, is a much more relevant issue than trying to figure out whether a public survey about how many people owned guns was more accurate than some other survey or poll.

The significance of the numeric and proportional increase in handguns is key to understanding what Lambert doesn't understand, which is that the whole demand for handguns has been driven by the same factor which has made many Americans believe that a gun is more of a benefit than a risk; namely, the idea of using a gun for self-defense. If I have one basic criticism of Lott's book, it is not that his regressions on right-to-carry (RTC) issuance and crime rates do not add up. Rather, it is that he should have used the growing interest in RTC and the liberalization of RTC laws as a proxy for the more important cultural shift in how Americans view the ownership and use of guns.

Lott argues that the spread of RTC laws and the issuance of RTC licenses creates the perception that more Americans are armed. And this perception on the part of the criminal population, is what turns criminals away from confronting their victims in the act of committing a crime, and instead makes criminals more likely to engage in anonymous crimes; i.e., crimes against property like burglary, where the odds of going up against an armed individual are not as great. Since his approach relies on assuming the existence of a *perception* about gun ownership on the part of evil-doers rather than whether a potential crime victim might have access to a gun, he might have made it more difficult for critics to attack his argument had he used the spread of R-T-C laws as a proxy for the ownership of guns.

131

The real strength of Lott's approach, however, is his attempt to correlate crime data with R-T-C at the county level, even though he often estimates state-level trends based on what he finds in county data within individual states. Lott was the first and remains the foremost exponent of understanding and explaining the drawbacks in gun research when the data which is used for developing any analysis of gun violence rests only on state-level trends. His comparison of the strengths and weaknesses of time-series versus cross-sectional evidence (pp. 20 *et. seq.* in *MGLC*) is cogent and clear, and his awareness of the necessity to probe the motives of people who decide to become self-defense gun owners is a powerful reminder that no amount of data can ever fully explain the ins and outs of the human mind.

In that respect, I conducted a limited, online survey which was answered by 231 respondents who were asked to participate only if they owned what they considered to be a 'self-defense' gun. Before getting to the specific issue of armed-self-defense, the respondents were required to answer some basic questions about their gun-owning history and personal demographics, the most common answer summarized here:

Q1 – How long have you been a gun owner? 75% said 15 years or more.

Q2 – Are you male or female? 97% were male.

Q3 – What is your age? 80% were over the age of 41.

Q4 – What kind of guns do you own? 88% owned both handguns and long guns.

Q5 – What was the last gun you acquired? Handguns – 63%, long guns – 36%.

Q6 – When did you acquire your last gun? Within a year – 66%.

Having established a basic profile of self-defense gun owners (male, ages 40 and above, long-time gun owners, has both long guns and handguns

132

around and added another gun to the household in the last year), the survey then got down to the specific experiences which motivated these individuals to think about gun ownership in terms of self-defense.

Q7 – Do you own a specific 'self-defense' gun? Yes – 97%.

Q8 – Have you or someone else in your home been the victim of a violent crime in the last 3 years? 5% said 'yes' but any positive response required a description of the event. Here they those descriptions:

Homicide

Rape

Niece attacked by ex-husband.

Break in.

My daughter had a released convicted sex predator stalk her.

Daughter's boyfriend shot at her. His missed thank goodness!

Yes, kicked in door wife couldn't get to gun range across street to neighbor. Now carries all around house

Sexual assault (Sister)

Kidnapped

Attempted robbery at a gas pump

Assault

Q9 – Does your self-defense gun make you less worried about being a crime victim? 79% said 'yes.'

All of the recent surveys which attempt to explain gun-owning behavior note the shift from owning guns for hunting and sport to owning guns for self-defense.[10] Notwithstanding the limitations of a survey that only captures responses from 230 participants, my survey is the first published

133

attempt to go in some degree of detail to try and understand not just why people own guns but what made them change their rationale for gun ownership and use from one type of behavior to another. The NRA, John Lott and everyone else who have been advocating RTC wouldn't have made a dent in the collective consciousness of gun owners had this consumer market not been receptive to this new idea.

When asked to describe whether the last gun they acquired was a hand gun or a long gun, all four age groups registered basically the same percentage (65%) who said that their last gun was a handgun. But while the 50+ age group said that they had acquired their most recent gun sometimes between one and five years, the younger age groups, particularly the age group of gun owners between 21 and 30, had mostly acquired their most recent gun within the previous 12 months; indeed, 96% of the 21 – 30 age group stated this recent acquisition to be the case.

In other words, what this survey appears to indicate (again, it is limited so therefore can only be a suggestive rather than definitive result, is that: 1) most of the individuals coming into the gun market for the first time will acquire a handgun; and, 2) experiencing violent crime is not as uncommon amongst this population as it is typical of the American population. In 2015, 0.40% of all Americans past age 12 were victims of violent crime.[11] In our survey, 5% of the respondents reported violent crimes, and even though the answers went back three years, dividing the responses equally over that time still brings the annual toll to be at least twice as high as what the *Bureau of Justice Statistics* reports for the country.

By confining their criticisms of John Lott's work to tendentious, nit-picking over the value of one kind of regression model or another, or simply using various forms of ad-hominem attacks, the critics of John Lott have managed to obscure not only the value of his research, but consciously or unconsciously push the argument away from his most salient point, namely, the degree to which Americans not only fear criminal threats, but have decided that a logical and positive response to those fears is to own and sometimes carry a gun.

Part of this unwillingness to face the implications of Lott's argument is based on the difficulty, admitted by everyone, of a fundamental issue of cognitive dissonance which everyone acknowledges but nobody has figured out how to solve. I refer here to the endless public opinion survey which find that the fear of crime within the general population appears to be much higher than the actual existence or experience of crime itself. So, for example, a Gallup poll published in 2016 showed that the percentage of Americans (53%) who worry "a great deal" about crime has now reached the highest level since 2001, having slowly declined to a low-point (39%) in 2014. Meanwhile, although violent crime rates have appeared to stabilize or even slightly increased since a near-50% decrease between 1995 and 2001, the public concern about violent criminality seems somewhat out of place. Not being able to figure out why people fear crime when crime rates remain low makes it seductively easy to assume the existence of the same kind of cognitive dissonant behavior when it come to the issue of guns.

But what our little survey clearly indicates is that acquiring a gun may not be such an unreal response to crime among the population which experiences or hears about criminal events first-hand. Here again is where Lott's research should be taken seriously by scholars who lean towards gun control, because his emphasis on county-level, rather than state-level numbers, is not only unique in this field, but is the only way to truly understand how, why and where people own self-defense guns.

Until and unless gun violence scholars begin to create research models which rest on the possibility that gun ownership may be a rational response to crime or at least a rational fear of crime, we are left on the one hand with Lott's work which presumes such rationality on behalf both gun owners and the criminals, and a complete avoidance of this presumption in the work of his Lott's critics. A recent example of how Lott's work is both abused and distorted by the failure of his scholarly critics to take issue with the main thrust of his ideas can be found in an op-ed piece written by a non-scholar who has compiled a massive database on gun violence research (which he refers to as a 'university') but is basically a gun-control activist and one of the leaders of the 'get Lott' group.[12]

The author of this piece, Devin Hughes, takes issue with Lott's argument that laws which require locking guns up or locking them away does not reduce accidental injuries from guns. Such laws, commonly referred to as child access prevention (CAP) laws, exist in multiple states, but Hughes cites the CDC-generated data on unintentional gun injuries with a degree of confidence that simply has no basis in truth. Precisely because the data which Hughes claims contradicts Lott's argument is aggregated only at the state level, it is not only unreliable, but for many states there are no numbers at all. Furthermore, none of the studies of unintentional gun injuries suffered by children even attempt to study whether the gun which caused the injury was left around unlocked for a period or was simply grabbed out of the hands of the gun-owning adult or was being used by a child whose behavior was being supervised by an adult. Absent such information, simply citing some inaccurate numbers about how many children are injured each year with guns doesn't prove or disprove what Lott is arguing, and therefore just adds another bit of mindless cacophony to what otherwise an argument should be based on valid evidence and facts.

I believe the reason that many gun-control advocates hate John Lott is because he serves as a convenient totem for this population's hatred and fear of guns. Which happens to be a legitimate fear that many people hold, and since they are enjoined from being able to act on that fear thanks to my late friend Antonin Scalia and his interpretation of 2nd-Amendment 'rights,' the fear turns into an anger and then a hatred of those people who appear to endorse the idea that not only can't we get rid of guns, but we shouldn't get rid of them because for many people guns serve a good cause.

I happen to think that the lack of reality is not a function of Lott's research, but is much more a reflection of why the gun-control movement has not been able to create a substantive, statutory framework which would reduce the violence caused by guns. The fact that certain states with large, non-gun owning majorities can impose stricter regulations on gun-owning minorities within their own jurisdictions does not say anything about the possibility of ever constructing a comprehensive, national framework in which the lethal products that kill and injure 125,000 people each year are simply proscribed from being available for everyday use. Such a development would obviously require the tacit, if not active support of the population which currently owns guns. This support will never be gained or even remotely considered by engaging in mindless and silly attacks on John Lott.

NOTES

1.The first paper is: J. Donohue and I. Ayers, "Nondiscretionary Concealed Weapons Law: A Case Study of Statistics, Standards of Proof, and Public Policy," *Yale Law School Legal Scholarship Repository*, Vol. 1, 1 (1999), pp. 1 – 27. I will refer to this paper as D & A – 1999. The second paper is: I. Ayers and J. Donohue, "Shooting Down the More Guns Less Crime Hypothesis," *Yale Law School Legal Scholarship Repository*, Vol. 1, 1 (2003), pp.1193-1312. I will refer to this paper as I & A – 2003.

2. "The impact of Legalized Abortion on Crime," *Quarterly Journal of Economics,* CXVI, 2 (May, 2001), pp. 379-420. Regarding Levitt's academic-entrepreneurial career, I am obviously referring to Freakonomics of which the best comment on the whole Levitt-Dubner approach is Elizabeth Kolbert's critique in *The New Yorker:* https://www.newyorker.com/magazine/2009/11/16/hosed.

3. Cf., *Firearms and Violence, A Critical Review* (Washington, D.C., 2005.) In 2017, Donohue appeared as an expert witness in *Flanagan v. Becerra,* a California case and stated that the panel had 'emphatically rejected' Lott's argument, which in fact the panel did not do. This quote is on Page 3 of

137

Donohue's deposition in this case:
http://blog.californiarighttocarry.org/wp-content/uploads/2016/08/45-8-Exhibit-7.pdf.

4. Oliver Roeder, et. al., *What Caused the Great Crime Decline?* (New York, Brennan Center for Justice, 2015.)
[5]

5. J. Lott, *More Guns, Less Crime, Understanding Crime and Gun Control Laws*, 3rd edn., (Chicago: 2010), p. xi.
[6]

6.J. Lott and D. Mustard, "Crime, Deterrence and Right-to-Carry Concealed Handguns," The Journal of Legal Studies Vol. 26, 1 (January, 1997), pp. 1 – 68.

7.https://pdfs.semanticscholar.org/6e39/24f3379ab98c9b64a602135d6c3fec8546bf.pdf

8. G. Kleck, Targeting Guns: *Firearms and their Control* (New York, 1997.) I also cite Kleck's Point Blank: *Guns and Violence in America* (New York, 2005.)

9.Kleck, Guns and Violence, p.48. ATF data from annual production report. For 2016 report: https://www.atf.gov/resource-center/docs/undefined/firearms-commerce-united-states-annual-statistical-update-2017/download.
10. D. Azrael, et. al., "The Stock and Flow of Firearms: Results from the 2015 National Firearms Survey," The Russell Sage Foundation Journal of the Social Sciences, Vol. 3, No. 5 (October, 2017) pp. 38 – 57.

11.https://www.bjs.gov/content/pub/pdf/cv15_sum.pdf.

12. http://thehill.com/opinion/civil-rights/390074-gun-control-that-works-safe-storage-saves-lives.

138

Study 8 - Gun Laws and Gun Violence.

In 1998 an economist named John Lott published a book, *More Guns, Less Crime*, in which he argued that violent crimes, particularly murder, were reduced in many jurisdictions which were issuing licenses that allowed private citizens to keep loaded guns either in their homes or on their person when they left their homes. At the time the book was first published, less than 30 states granted their residents an unrestricted right to carry a gun on their person, a number which has now been extended to 42 states, and all 50 states now allow residents to keep a loaded gun in their home without prior approval beyond the standard, law-abiding criteria which has been recognized since 1968 and given Constitutional protection since 2008.[1]

Prior to Lott's book, which became something of a standard point-of-reference groups promoting gun ownership, public health researchers had begun identifying the risks of gun ownership and had published several substantial studies which showed that access to a firearm increased injury rates from guns, regardless of whether the gun was being carried outside or simply stored inside the home. These studies also did not differentiate between guns that were safely stored (i.e., locked or locked away) but simply defined the presence of a gun to be a health risk.[2]

The debate between gun risk versus gun benefits quickly tilted in favor of the latter narrative, with the percentage of Americans (according to Gallup) who supported less restrictive gun laws sliding from 78% in 1990 to 42% in 2011. But in the past several years the gun-risk argument appears to be gaining momentum, from 47% calling for stricter laws in 2015 to 67% in March 2018, the highest support that more restrictive laws have registered since 1993.

This shift in public opinion is obviously a reflection of the degree to which gun rampages costing multiple lives have occurred over the past six

140

months. First there was the October 2017 shooting in Las Vegas, which
resulted in 59 deaths, then 26 dead in a Texas church in November, then
17 killed at Parkland, Florida in February, 2018, with the Parkland
massacre unleashing a virtual tidal wave of media attention which was
followed by more than 800 demonstrations against gun violence in
virtually every state as well as overseas.[3]

Were it not for the fact that gun control remains a toxic political issue for
Republicans, along with the fact that a President now sits in the Oval
Office who proclaims himself to be a strong supporter of 2nd-Amendment
'rights,' there is no doubt that some kind of additional gun-control law
would be moving through the Congress and possibly ending up on a
different Chief Executive's desk. As it is, several measures in support of
gun ownership which were slowly but surely advancing towards the
legislative finish line (e.g., national concealed-carry, removing silencers
from the restricted NFA list) now appear to be stalled, if not for the
moment dead. If the early election polls hold true through November and
Congress turns from red to blue, you can be sure that an effort to push a
new law restricting or regulating gun ownership will come to pass.

If we continue to follow in general terms the disclaimer in the 2008 Heller
opinion that government has the authority to regulate guns, the argument
over regulations will continue with gun-control advocates citing study
after study which has found a positive correlation between more legal
restrictions over gun ownership resulting in less violence caused by guns.[5]

Of course, the simplest and most efficient way to reduce gun violence
would be to get rid of the guns, or at least make it extremely difficult for
the most lethal types of weapons to find their way into civilian hands. This
was how Australia reduced the threat of mass shootings; the government
simply banned the ownership of all assault rifles, one of which had been
used in a 1996 shooting which claimed 35 lives and injured 23 more. Not
only did the entire regulatory system become restrictive following this
event, but the government bought back roughly 20% of all legally-owned

141

firearms, some 600,000 semi-automatic rifles and shotguns, the result being a complete absence of rampage shootings from then until now.[4]

Given political reality however and the fact that such a complete disarming of the civilian population would never take place in the United States, the mitigating influence of laws over gun violence is considered by gun-control groups to be the most effective way to reduce the rate of gun injuries while, at the same time, giving lip service to the Constitutional protection afforded personally-owned guns.

The Argument: More Laws = Less Guns.

The formative, peer-reviewed study which claims that more laws equals less gun violence was done by Eric Fleegler and associates, who correlated gun-injury rates and gun laws in all 50 states for the years 2007 through 2010.[5] The researchers used CDC data on gun violence and used Brady to determine the number of gun laws in each state. Conclusion: "A higher number of firearm laws in a state are associated with a lower rate of firearm fatalities in the state, overall and for suicides and homicides individually."

But before we look at the data behind this conclusion which shows an apparent correlation between gun laws and gun violence; i.e., more gun laws/regulations equal less gun violence, we should first spend some time discussing the laws themselves. There are two main resources used for such research contained on the websites run by the Brady campaign and the Giffords group. Both these sites rank states in terms of the degree to which guns are regulated in what are considered restrictions that promote safety and reduce violence caused by guns; the sites then compare these rankings to how each state fares in terms of the rate of gun violence registered within.[6] The national map colored by the Brady rankings looks like this:

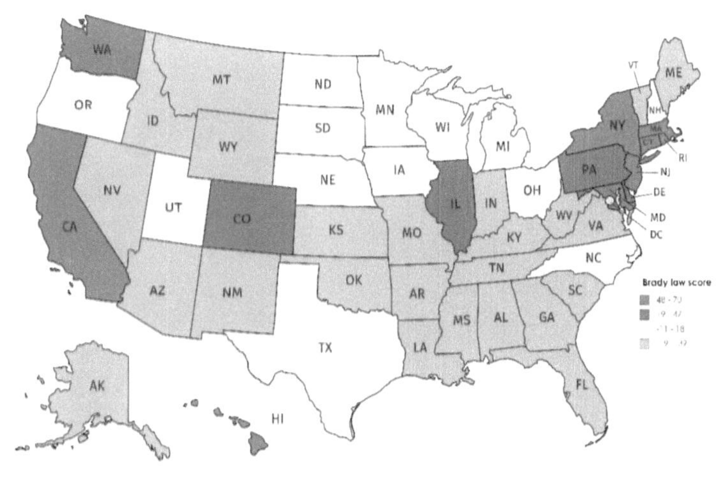

States with the highest rankings, i.e., the most comprehensive gun laws are colored red, states somewhere in the middle are blue followed by yellow, states with few or no gun laws are green. The average for all states is between scores for yellow and blue. In other words, the safest states are red, the least safe are green, and if you live in a 'green' state, according to Brady, you are living in a place with little or no regulations covering guns. If you live in a red state, on the other hand, when it comes to gun violence, legally speaking, you should be safe.

Here is the same map according to the Giffords group:

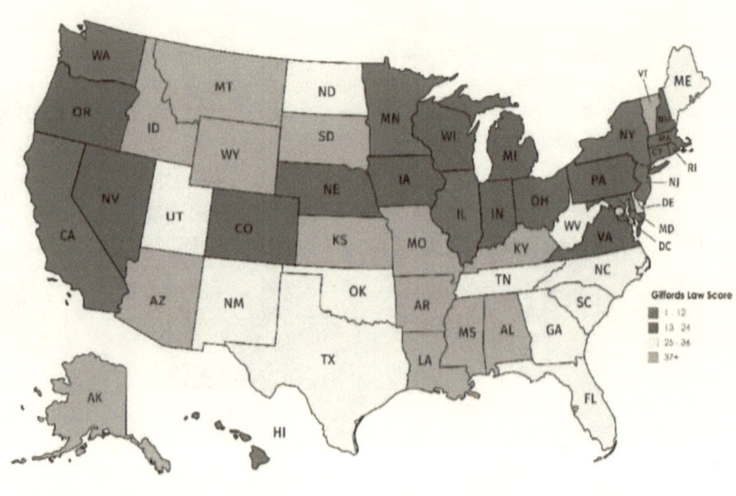

Note that the Giffords group lumps twice as many states in the 'best' and above-average categories as are found in Brady, while the 'worst' states include fewer states from the Deep South. Indeed, Brady finds that almost twice as many states have the fewest number of gun restrictions – there are 24 green states on the Brady map, only 14 on the map representing the data from the Giffords group.

Much of the difference between the way in which the two organizations identify and rank states has to do with how they evaluate gun laws in each locality. The Giffords group bases its analysis on eight specific categories covering threats to public safety:

    1. Child-access prevention laws;
    2. Concealed-carry regulations;
    3. Dangerous person disarmament;
    4. Mental health reporting;
    5. Open carry;
    6. Comprehensive background checks;
    7. Domestic abusers;

8. Waiting periods for gun transfers.

Within each category, state laws are rated strong, weak, or no rating because a law covering that issue doesn't exist. The only state of all 50 states which has a strong law for every category is California, which gave the Golden State a grade of 'A.' Seven other states – CT, MA, MD, NJ, NY, HI) were rated 'A-' and four more states – IL, RI, WA, DE – were rated 'B+' or 'B.' Yet New York only has 3 of 8 categories with laws rated as 'strong,' whereas Delaware had 4 strong legal categories, but New York is rated at A- and Delaware is rated as 'B.' For that matter, Rhode Island has 6 legal categories rated as strong but received a 'B+,' slightly lower than the score given to New York.

Obviously, the Giffords group is basing its gun-law scorecard not just on the existence of relevant laws, but the value of certain laws as being more important for reducing violence caused by guns. Here is how this methodology is described by the Giffords group:

> Our decades of experience working with legislators and advocates on tried and true solutions, alongside our development of new model laws, allows us to evaluate the relative strength of each policy and create a comprehensive grading system. We take away points for dangerous laws that play fast and loose with public safety, such as allowing people to carry concealed, loaded guns in public without a permit. After points are tallied, we assign letter grades based on the point total and rank the states in order from the highest score to the lowest.

I find it rather amusing that an organization which was founded in 2012 refers to itself as having 'decades' of experience in gun-control laws. Now to be fair, the Giffords group probably relied on the work of another organization, the California-based Legal Community Against Violence, which was founded in 1993 and merged with the Giffords Group in 2016. And if the Giffords group wants to pretend that their 'decades' of experience can somehow be used to disguise the fact that nowhere do they actually explain how and why they rank various gun laws and use those rankings to create a list of 'good' versus 'bad' states, so be it. The bottom line is that their gun-law scorecard shouldn't be considered a scholarly tool.

On the other hand, the Brady Campaign's scorecard not only contains a very detailed description of every gun law on which their state ratings are based, it also includes a numerical weighting system which allows the reader to understand how Brady rated different gun laws by their effectiveness in reducing gun violence rates. This rating system is entirely absent from the gun-law report issued by the Giffords group. Rather, the reader is asked to accept their methodology based on the 'decades' of experience in evaluating gun laws and the effects of those laws.

The Critique.

There is only one slight problem, however, with the explanatory details provided by Brady; namely, that their judgements about the efficacy of various gun laws and regulations for reducing gun violence are, in most cases, based on no substantive data or valid data at all. For example, a state is granted 25 points for requiring comprehensive background checks on all gun transfers, but there has yet to be a single piece of research which shows that when a state moves from the current system which only requires background checks for the initial sale of a gun to any kind of comprehensive system, that gun violence goes down. The Brady scorecard counts 7 states as being awarded 25 points for this law, one of those seven states being New York.

In 2013 New York State passed the Safe Act which, among other provisions, extended background checks to all gun transfers within the Empire State. In 2014, according to the CDC, the gun-violence rate per 100,000 New York residents was 4.36. In 2015 the rate dropped to 4.25. So far, so good. But in 2016 the rate went back up to 4.52, higher than it

146

was in 2013, the year prior to the passage of the SAFE Act. In Colorado, another state that passed a comprehensive background check law in 2013, the gun-violence has increased by 25 percent (!) from 2013 to 2016, in numeric terms from 11.45 to 14.31 per 100,000 state residents. So, for these two states, Brady is awarding the maximum number of points for a law which cannot be said to have had any mitigating impact on gun violence whatsoever.

On the other hand, Colorado loses 6 points because it does not grant law enforcement discretion in handing out concealed-carry permits. In Colorado, if an applicant passes a background check that individuals gets concealed-carry privileges, like it or not. According to the Violence Policy Center, of the 1,229 fatalities committed by concealed-carry holders (including suicides) since 2007, exactly five of these deaths involved Coloradans with the right to legally walk around with a gun. This happens to be .004% of the total carnage aggregated by the VPC since 2007. The population of Colorado happens to be 1.75% of the total national population. In other words, there is no statistical correlation between the state's non-discretionary concealed-carry law and violence committed by such individuals at all.

Rather than go through the gun laws of every state which would show a similar discordance between laws and gun-violence rates as we have found in the case of Colorado, the map below is based on the latest gun-violence data as published by the CDC:

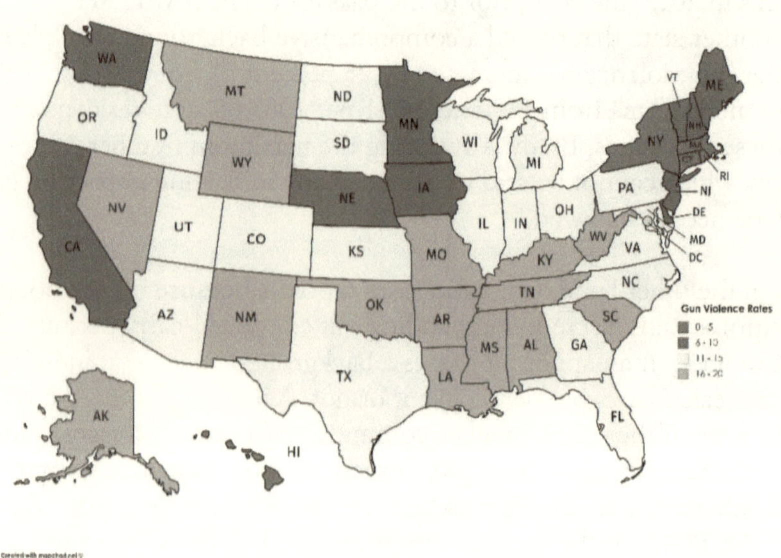

Compare this map to the Brady map on Page 126 above. Note that the only states which receive a high score from Brady and register the lowest rates of gun violence are New York, Connecticut, Rhode Island and Massachusetts. California is awarded the highest Brady score, but its gun-violence rate is higher than the other high-scoring Brady states as well. Illinois Colorado, Washington and Pennsylvania ranked just below the top five Brady states, but Illinois, Colorado and Pennsylvania all have gun-violence rates above the national media rate. Iowa, Minnesota and Nebraska all have below-average Brady scores, yet all have gun-violence rates that are lower than the national media rate.

If there is, indeed, a causal connection between more gun laws and less gun violence, it simply cannot be said that this relationship is directly, or perhaps even indirectly caused by state-by-state differences in the strength and comprehensiveness of gun laws. There is, however, another factor which might prove to represent a more plausible research methodology into the factors behind more and less gun violence, which I call the degree

148

of state-level business activity tied to guns. In other words, can we find a correlation between gun violence rates and how many guns circulate in any given state?

Gun Violence and Guns.

The relationship between gun violence levels and access to firearms is, in fact, the most credible research on gun violence conducted by public health researchers, although perhaps the best presentation of this argument was made by a legal scholar, Frank Zimring, in 1999.[7] Building on his own research, as well as substantial monographic research by public health scholars (Kellerman, Rivara, et. al.,) Zimring persuasively showed that the most plausible factor differentiating violent crime in the U.S. from similar crime categories in other Western countries was the availability of guns.[8]

The problem confronting public health researchers and gun-control advocates, however, is that while they can retrieve data on gun injuries from the CDC on a state-by-state basis, no such data exists when it comes to identifying the location of guns. At best, researchers derive estimates based on what they refer to as 'proxies,' such as the research by Michael Siegel and others who use gun-suicide rates to approximate general ownership of guns.[9] But such attempts to approximate the geographical location of guns should not be used as a basis for making assumptions about the relationship of gun access to any issue involving gun laws for two reasons:

1. Guns have a shelf life far beyond any other consumer item, and since there was no gun registration regulations prior to 1968, by which time there were already more than 100 million guns in private hands, it should be presumed that most of those guns are somewhere still lying around.[10]

149

2. While the ATF has published the monthly NICS background checks on a state-by-state basis since 1999, the data fails to disclose how many checks represent new guns as opposed to checks on used guns, the latter not reflecting any addition to the overall civilian gun stock, but rather, the recycling of previously-sold guns.

There is, however, a database that can be used, with care and caution, to estimate not the specific number of guns found in every state. But the degree of gun business and gun activity which occurs in every state. I am referring to the monthly ATF listing of active gun dealer licenses, whose numbers can be used to differentiate gun access in the various states.

Guns happen to be the only consumer product for which a federal license is required to operate within the consumer market; more important, every licensee must maintain accurate records of every gun bought and sold. While the ATF does not track the actual volume of gun sales in any shop, a per-capita analysis of gun dealers on a state-by-state basis tells us a great deal about the relative degree of guns sitting in each state.

The ability to use federal firearm license (FFL) numbers for understanding the location of civilian-owned guns must be undertaken with a great deal of caution and nuance, for the simple reason that the vast majority of FFL-holders don't actually engage in the business of selling guns. As of December, 2017, the ATF listed 118,850 federal licensees whose license allowed them to receive and ship a gun across a state line. How many of these license-holders needed a state or local license to engage in the gun business is simply not known, but we can assume that most of the individuals who went to the trouble and cost of becoming federal licensees would also become licensed at the state and/or local level if such licensing was also required in order to deal in guns.

Of these 118,850 FFL-holders, 56,199 held what is referred to as 01 licenses, which means they could not only buy and ship guns across state lines but could also sell or transfer guns to persons other than themselves. Another 7,825 FFL-holders had what is referred to as 02 licenses, which are given to dealers who are also licensed pawn shops, and often receive guns not because they have been purchased, but because they have been given (and might then be returned) in pawn. Finally, the remaining 54,826 FFL-holders (aside from the 15,334 licensees who manufacture or import guns and ammunition but cannot sell any of their products to specific consumers without also holding a 01 or 02 license) possess a Curio & Relics license which allows them to bring across a state line any firearm as long as it is 50 years old, but they can only transfer these guns to other FFL-holders, usually 03 holders like themselves.

The media loves to run scare stories saying that there are more gun dealers than there are Starbucks or Burger King stores, but this is simply not true.[11] The fact that an individual holds the 01 FFL license doesn't obligate that person to actually be in the business of selling guns. And even though the government has been trying, without success, to figure out a valid definition of the phrase 'in business' when it comes to buying and selling guns, the fact is that most FFL-holders are gun hobbyists for whom the initial $200 licensing fee (valid for three years and then renewable for $90) will amount to a much greater savings than purchasing several guns from a retail dealer, as opposed to being able to buy guns direct from wholesalers who will ship to anyone in the United States as long as they possess the requisite FFL.

How do we differentiate between 01 licensees who conduct a real gun business, as opposed to 01 license-holders who are hobbyists wanting to take advantage of the difference in retail and wholesale prices of guns? The most credible method would be to send a survey request to every FFL-holder asking them to divulge the degree to which they actually engage in the gun business, which was the method employed by Garen Wintemute who estimated that 18% of all 01 FFL-holders sold 50 or more guns every year.[12]

151

I tried to estimate the number of 01 licensees using a different method which involved analyzing the entire dealer list on the Smith & Wesson website for all authorized dealers in three state: Massachusetts, Rhode Island and Connecticut. The virtue of this methodology lies in the fact that Smith & Wesson has aggressively built an online dealer database as a way to encourage to patronize gun shops where the company's products are found, and the most comprehensive listings are in the states closest to the gun maker's factory itself. As of December 2017, there were 885 active 01 licenses in those three states; there were 89 Smith & Wesson gun dealers in those same states. In other words, 10% of the 01 licensees were engaged in the business of selling guns.

Our findings from looking at the distribution of Smith & Wesson dealers are not that different from what Wintemute found for his study of the business practices of FFL-licensees who sold at least one gun per week. But the fact that someone doesn't conduct a retail gun business doesn't necessarily mean that the individual doesn't own guns and move his personal inventory into the hands of others either through trades or private sales. And even though the latest estimate on non-NICS gun transfers finds that such activity represents only 20% of all movement of guns, if the FBI conducts an average of 12 million to 13 million background checks every year, the non-regulated transfer number would still be in excess of two to three million guns.[13]

Thus, knowing the per capita number of FFL-holders in each state is a valid method for estimating the degree of gun activity in each state, particularly if we dd to the 01 number the amount of 03 licenses issued in each state. Again, 03 license holders cannot use their license to transfer guns to anyone except other 03 licensees in any state. But the number of 03 licenses in any jurisdiction is a very good proxy for determining the relative level of gun ownership and interest/involvement in guns. If we combine 01 and 03 licenses and then create a state-by-state analysis of per capita licenses of both types, we get a map which looks like this:

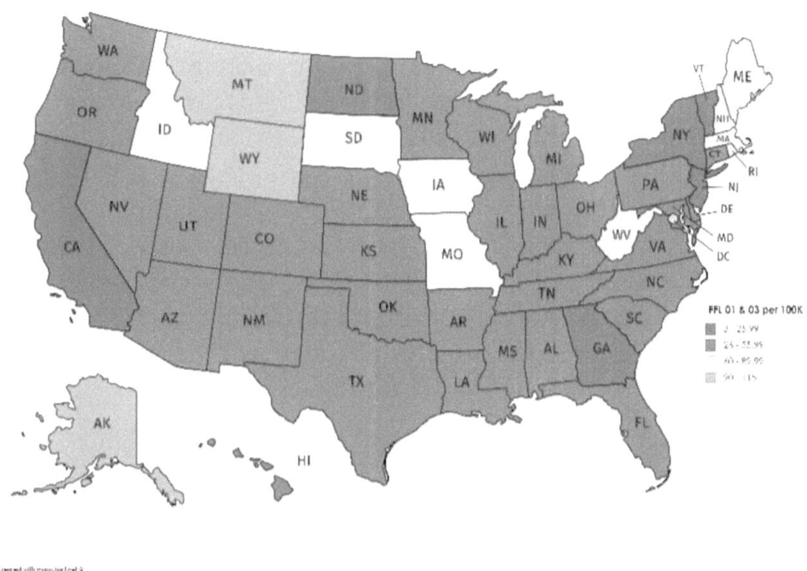

With the exception of Georgia and North Dakota, the only states whose per capita FFL numbers rank substantially below the national median (red and blue) are basically the same states that receive a maximum 'safe' score from Brady because of strong and comprehensive gun laws. The states with the highest per capita license numbers (yellow and green) are all states, with the exception of Massachusetts and Connecticut, which Brady ranks as 'unsafe.'

Obviously, states with restrictive gun laws would also tend to be states that impose more regulations over conducting a business in guns. And such states would also have lower per capita gun ownership rates, but this brings us to the classic chicken-and-egg issue which regression analysis does not necessarily give us a clear pathway to solve. In other words, when we find differences in gun violence rates from state to state, are we looking at the effects of more gun laws or simply the fact that such states contain less guns?

Chances are we are looking at both. And here is where the argument over whether gun laws reduce gun violence needs to be considered from a more nuanced point of view. Because if the experience of product regulation is any guide, there is no doubt that finding the correct balance between government regulation and market growth is, at best, an uncertain task.[14] The regulatory problem is complicated with respect to guns because our regulatory system for firearms is based primarily on regulating not the products themselves, but the behavior of the consumers who purchase, own and use the guns. Anyone who thinks that regression analysis can unerringly connect the outcome of human behavior to legal change is taking a giant leap of faith whose results often cannot be sustained.[15]

Conclusion

The purpose of this paper was not to raise doubts about the need to regulate firearm in an effective and positive way; positive meaning that we pass laws that will have the desired effect. And the problem with the current regulatory system covering guns which we first introduced in 1968, is that it focuses primarily on behavior of gun owners with concerns about the existence of the products themselves to be relegated to second best.

It seems to be self-evident that the more any product is found within the general population, the greater are the odds that it might be used in an unsafe way, particularly a product whose very design and use can so easily function in a manner which causes harm. Which is why the community that studies and advocates for more effective gun controls needs to take the size and activity of the gun market into account when trying to figure out whether a legal change will have the desired effect. Hopefully, this paper creates some pathways for helping researchers to achieve that goal.

NOTES.

1.2008 Heller, etc.

2.Kellerman, A., et. al., "Gun Ownership as a Risk Factor for Homicide in the Home," New England Journal of Medicine, 329 (October 7, 1993), 1084-1091.

3. https://www.nytimes.com/interactive/2018/03/22/us/politics/march-for-lives-demonstrations.html.

4.http://www.slate.com/blogs/crime/2012/12/16/gun_control_after_connecticut_shooting_could_australia_s_laws_provide_a.html.

5.https://jamanetwork.com/journals/jamainternalmedicine/fullarticle/1661390.

6. For Brady: http://www.crimadvisor.com/data/Brady-State-Scorecard-2014.pdf. For Giffords: http://lawcenter.giffords.org/scorecard2016/.

7. Zimring, F., and Hawkins, G., *Crime Is Not the Problem – Lethal Violence in America* (New York: Oxford University Press, 1999).

8. fn. 2, op. cit.

9. M. Siegel, et. al., "The Relationship Between Gun Ownership and Firearm Homicide Rates in the United States, 1981–2010," American Journal of Public Health 103, 11 (November 1, 2013), 2098 – 2015.

10. G. Kleck, Point Blank, Guns and Violence in America, (New York: DeGruyter, 1991), p. 49.

11. Typical example of such stories: https://www.businessinsider.com/gun-dealers-stores-mcdonalds-las-vegas-shooting-2017-10.

12. G. Wintemute, "Firearms Licensee Characteristics Associated with Sales of Crime- Involved Firearms and Denied Sales: Findings from the Firearms Licensee Survey," *The Russell Sage Foundation Journal of the Social Sciences,* 3, 5 (October, 2017), 58 – 74.

13. http://annals.org/aim/fullarticle/2595892/firearm-acquisition-without-background-checks-results-national-survey.

14. https://www.innovationpolicyplatform.org/content/product-market-regulation.

15. R. Berk, Regression Analysis, A Constructive Critique (London: Sage Publications, 2004), p. 97 et. seq.

Study 9 - Murder and Guns.

Who gets murdered when someone kills someone else with a gun? This isn't as easy a question to figure out as you may think. Even though the CDC tries to keep track of all deaths so that the Census can then keep track of changes in the overall population count, we do not have a system which guarantees that the state-level entities who collect health-related data and then allegedly transmit that data to the federal level either: a) collect all relevant data, or, b) transmit it in a manner consistent with how the data is then aggregated by the federal agencies responsible for tracking these events.

In addition to the issue of how relevant information is collected, aggregated and transmitted, violent death creates another significant problem insofar as it is the only type of mortality event whose incidence is important to the workings of two, very separate and very different constituencies – medicine and law enforcement. Not only do these two entities deal with violent death differently in terms of response to the event itself, they also use very different methodological approaches to frame the research conducted on how and why such events occur.

First, let's look at numbers. According to the CDC, 15,872 people were homicide victims in 2014, of whom 11,008 were killed with guns.[1] Although I will compare 2015 numbers from different medical sources below, for the initial comparison between law enforcement and medical records, the most recent year we can use is 2014. That year, the FBI recorded 13,472 murders, guns being used in 8,124 of those events.[2] How come 2,400 dead bodies were counted by medical authorities but somehow missed by the cops? As for guns used by one person to kill someone else, between the medical versus the police number, some 3,000 guns seem to have disappeared.

How do we account for such numerical differences between two government agencies that are allegedly looking at the same thing? The
158

most obvious answer, and certainly a substantial explanation for how and why these numbers are so out of whack, is that the CDC database is built from reports from state-level health authorities who rely largely on death certificates filed by whomever a particular jurisdiction certifies to be responsible for this task.

The FBI, on the other hand, builds their data from arrests, which are not only less than a complete listing for any serious crime, but are rarely updated by matching the arrest record to a court adjudication which might take place several years following the event. Additionally, both CDC and FBI explicitly state that their numbers are what they refer to as 'reliable estimates,' with the emphasis on the latter word, not the former.

This data discrepancy would be inconsequential if the estimates from CDC and FBI differed only to a slight degree. But the fact that these estimates at both the national and state-by-state level are often in disagreement by more than 30% is cause for concern for two reasons. First, the CDC data is used unhesitatingly by public health gun-violence researchers who only raise the issue of data consistency and veracity when the CDC itself raises the issue. Second, the medical data is also used by the gun violence prevention (GVP) community in addressing the problem of gun violence either to support a particular regulatory initiative or to raise public awareness, or both.

The data lacunae becomes even more pronounced when we try to match up CDC numbers with more specific medical data which is supposed to give us a more granular portrait of what gun violence is all about. The basic data source for information about all injuries is the CDC's National Center for Injury Prevention and Control, which can be accessed online in the WISQARS database. The more granular data is allegedly found in two other collections which feed off of the CDC: the WONDER database and the National Violent Death Reporting System, a.k.a. NVDRS.[3]

The WONDER database is advertised as an "easy-to-use, menu-driven system that makes the information resources of the Centers for Disease

Control and Prevention (CDC) available to public health professionals and the public at large." For purposes of the kind of research on which this paper is based, WONDER allows one to go directly to the data based on 'Injury Intent and Mechanism,' so that one can group all the data on gun murders and break the data down to its corresponding parts.

Unfortunately, the moment one goes below the state-level categories used to search the CDC-WISQARS collection, the granularity basically disappears. For example, the WONDER database can be searched data on gun murders not just by state but on a county-level basis, a very important function given the disparity between urban and on-urban violence in many states. Except when one calls up the 2015 county data for New York State, only 11 of New York's 62 counties are listed, and the numbers for 5 of the 11 counties are stated to be 'unreliable.' Here is how WISQARS maps the New York State county data for gun murders:

Crude Rate for New York

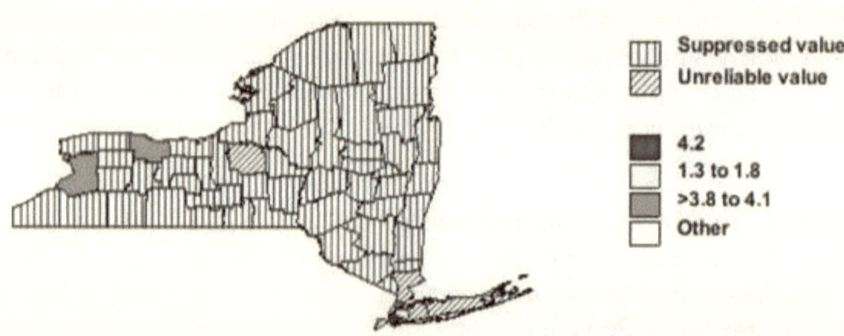

In other words, it's useless. Things don't get any better when we try to mine data out of the NVDRS, if only because this database currently draws from only 26 states whose total population is roughly half the population of the entire United States. But even when we try to compare CDC versus NVDRS numbers for the same states, things don't add up.

Note that when we look at CDC and NVDRS the comparison is based on 2915 numbers, whereas when we compare medical to law enforcement numbers we move back to 2014. This is because the 2014 NVDRS numbers are too scant (covering only 20 states) to make any valid national comparisons.

For 2015, gun homicides in the NVDRS totaled 4,114, but CDC counts the same 26 states as experiencing 5,315 gun murders that year, a discrepancy of more than 20 percent. I will return to the issue of validating murder data further on, but for the moment let's just say that I am not convinced that using public health, as opposed to criminal data, has any basis in reliable fact beyond the degree to which higher numbers make the problem appear to be worse than it might really be.

Notwithstanding the data issues above, here is what we know, or at least think we know, about who gets shot and killed each year by someone else using a gun. Of the 12,979 victims of gun homicide in 2015, the CDC says that 11,029 (85%) were males, 1,950 were females. This adds up to 13,029, which means that 50 gun-homicide victims were either hermaphrodites or somehow changed sexual orientation between when they were shot and when the information about their death was sent to the CDC.

Now let's look at age. Of all the gun-homicide victims counted by the CDC, 9,388 or 72%, were between the ages of 15 and 39. This group registered a per-100,000 death rate of 8.68, twice the rate of the country as a whole. Or to put it another way, deduct the 15 – 39 age group from the national number, and the rate for all gun homicides whose victims were outside the 15 – 39 age cohort is 1.69.

We know that gun violence and violence of all types is found overwhelmingly among adolescents and younger men, but if we drill down to the state level we again find that the numbers are more weak than strong. Less than half the states listed in the C DC give reliable numbers for all age cohorts between 15 – 34, and when we compare the CDC to the NVDRS, the discrepancy gets even worse. New York State, for example, counts 5% more gun homicides for the cohorts 15 – 44, but gives no reliable data for any cohorts above or below the 15 – 44 age groups.

Now let's turn to the elephant in the living room, namely, the issue of race. This is a particularly toxic problem within the gun-control community, not only because some of the most notorious gun murders involved Black victims and White shooters, such as the Martin – Zimmerman event, but inter-racial gun murders often involve shooters who happen to be cops; e.g., the killings of Michael Brown and Philando Castile. Like it or not, gun violence, particularly homicidal gun violence, appears to be disproportionately experienced within the minority communities, and any issue touching on the socio-economic disparity between Blacks and Whites is always treated gingerly, if discussed at all.

Meanwhile, what the public health data reveals about the racial component of gun murders is also less than exact. Again using 2015 from the CDC, total gun murders of White victims counted 5,013, Blacks were 7,615, the per-100K rate for African-Americans (16.10) being more than seven times higher than the White rate (2.07.) In the case of Blacks, the age cohorts 15 – 39 comprise 81% of total gun deaths; for Whites the cohort has to be widened to ages 15 through 54 before 80% of all gun deaths occur. When we move to NVDRS we can't validate the CDC data because none of the 26 NVDRS states break down racial gun deaths by age cohort at all.

What we are left with in the measurements of gun homicide used by public health researchers is a dataset from the CDC which gives overall numbers at least 20% higher than either data aggregated by WONDER or NVDRS; the CDC data routinely adopted without question by virtually every gun-control organization around.[4]

How come the data which creates the public health and GVP narratives about gun violence is never based on what is published by the FBI? Primarily because the FBI-UCR estimates are even lower than what can be gleaned from the CDC, please reference my comments on Page 2 above. But what if the FBI data turns out to be actually more accurate than what we get from the CDC? I'll start answering that question by first reviewing what both agencies explain how they collect and analyze the numbers for gun-homicide deaths.

The CDC collects its national data by aggregating state-level data from the National Vital Statistics System (NVSS) which is the CDC-based agency, the National Center for Health Statistics (NCHS,) which transmits data on births and deaths to the Census, so that we know how many people live in the United states, or at least we hope we know. But here is where any degree of uniformity in terms of record-keeping begins to break down, because the data gathered by the NCHS comes from "contracts between NCHS and vital registration systems operated in the various jurisdictions legally responsible for the registration of vital events – births, deaths, marriages, divorces, and fetal deaths." And these 'various jurisdictions' tend to be state-level agencies whose degree of technical competence, record-keeping diligence and data-maintenance technologies differs considerably from place to place.

What this all boils down to is when we talk about anything medically-related to causes of death, particularly violent death, we are looking at estimates, not necessarily true facts. Which is the same problem we confront using data published by the FBI. The basic difference between CDC and FBI, however, is that the latter agency draws its data only from one source; i.e., reports from non-federal police agencies throughout the United States, whereas the former draws data from a variety of sources (hospitals, medical examiners, funeral directors) who may or may not be necessarily using the same definitions of methodologies in determining or reporting the causes of deaths.

The lack of a set of consistent definitions for reporting crime has also been the chief criticism of the Uniform Crime Reports, but this seems to be, at best, an incidental problem when we talk about murder because either the victim of this particular crime is alive or dead. And even though

163

much has been made recently about the undercounting of cop-caused deaths, both the FBI and the CDC distinguish between homicides which are considered crimes, as opposed to deaths in which the perpetrator can demonstrate just cause.

In 2015 the FBI says there were 15,696 crimes considered to be 'murder and nonnegligent manslaughter,' a number which is then reduced by roughly 15% when these crimes are quantified in terms of age, race, gender, weapon or anything else. This number is roughly 12% below the same-year number given by the CDC, but the difference between the two reports jumps to 25% when we look at the number of murders committed with guns. According to the CDC, in 2015 there were 12,979 gun murders, the FBI only counts 9,616. The FBI figure, however, is based on 13,455 total murders, the CDC counts 17,793, the percentage of gun murders reported by both agencies being almost exactly the same. And the percentage of gun murders reported by the 6 NVDRS reporting states is also basically the same.

Is the degree of similarity between the FBI and the CDC for the proportion of murders involving the use of guns also found when we disassemble the murder numbers using other sub-categories such as gender and race? According to the CDC, 3,519 women, or 20% of all 17,793 victims were murdered in 2015. The FBI says that of 13,455 murders in 2015, females were the victims 21% of the time. Again, the overall numbers differ by 25%, but the proportion of male to female victims is almost the same. For the 26 NVDRS states reporting for 2015, the gender breakdown was also 20% for females, 80% for males.

The racial breakdown between law enforcement versus medical data is also exactly the same, even though the raw numbers again are much higher when reported by the CDC. In 2015, White homicide victims in the CDC report were 45% of the whole; the FBI says the White proportion of murder victims was 44% - take your pick. The 26 states that reported to the NVDRS had a White-Black breakdown of 38 – 58 percent, but recall

164

that NVDRS doesn't count a number of states (FL, AL, AR, LA, MO, CA) with higher-than-average murder rates.

Finally, when we compare distribution by age cohorts, the same proportions appear. For the CDC, 10,919 homicide victims in 2015 were between the ages of 17 and 39 which accounted for 61% of all murders that year. The FBI reports that 8,408 murder victims were between ages 17 and 39, which happens to be 62% of all homicide deaths in 2015. In sum, both medical and law enforcement data reveals that 70% of all homicide victims were killed with a gun; that four out of five victims were males, that three out of five victims were between the ages of 17 and 39, and the ratio of White to Black victims in both datasets is the same. So if the gender, age and type of weapon breakdown is the same for the data from both medicine and the cops, how do we explain the 20% difference in overall homicide numbers, a difference which might be even greater if we had national data from the NVDRS?

A possible answer to the gap between CDC and FBI murder numbers may be found in a recent study which found that 20% of the shootings classified by the CDC as homicides were, in fact, accidental shootings where there was no intentional behavior at all.[5] This determination was made by examining much more detailed data in the NVDRS. The study only looked at 183 cases covering children aged 0 -14 from 2005 to 2012. But while the sample is limited both by age cohorts and by the small number of participating states, the reasons why causes of death were misclassified – shooting was considered intentional when it wasn't, jurisdictional law required the death be listed as a homicide – would also apply to shooting injuries regardless of the victims's age.

While other studies have also found that unintentional gun deaths may be overreported (a more frequent occurrence with suicide rather than homicide,) the bottom line is that the medical numbers being used by GVP organizations and advocates to create the current narrative about the extent of gun violence should be regarded with caution and care.

NOTES

1. The CDC numbers can be accessed at https://www.cdc.gov/injury/wisqars/fatal.html.

2. The FBI numbers can be accessed at https://ucr.fbi.gov/.

3. https://wonder.cdc.gov/; https://www.cdc.gov/violenceprevention/nvdrs/index.html.

4. http://www.bradycampaign.org/key-gun-violence-statistics.

5. D. Hemenway & S. Solnick, "Children and unintentional firearm death," *Injury Epidemiology,* Vol. 2, no. 1 (Dec.,2015): https://www.ncbi.nlm.nih.gov/ pmc/articles/ /PMC4602049/.

Guns in America

1. Guns for Good Guys, Guns for Bad Guys

2. Hunters in the Wilderness

3. Because They're Assholes

4. The Great American Gun Argument

5. Gun Trafficking in America

6. The Myth of the Armed Citizen

7. Sandy Hook: A Man Sold A Gun

8. Confessions of a Gun Nut

9. Gun Notes – Research on Guns